Ryuho Okawa, founder and spiritual leader of the Institute for Research in Human Happiness (IRH), has devoted his life to the exploration of the spirit world and ways to happiness.

He was born in 1956 in Tokushima, Japan. After graduating from the University of Tokyo, he joined a major Tokyo-based trading house and studied international finance at the Graduate Center of the City University of New York. In 1986 he renounced his business career and established the IRH.

He has been designing IRH spiritual workshops for people from all walks of life, from teenagers to business executives. He is known for his wisdom, compassion and commitment to educating people to think and act in spiritual and religious ways. The members of the IRH follow the path he teaches, ministering to people who need help by spreading his teachings.

He is the author of many books and periodicals, including *The Laws of the Sun*, *The Golden Laws*, *The Laws of Eternity*, and *The Starting Point of Happiness*. He has also produced successful feature-length films (including animations) based on his works.

For further information on the Institute for Research in Human Happiness please visit www.irhpress.co.jp.

By the same author

The Challenge of
THE MIND

A Practical Approach to the
Essential Buddhist Teaching
of Karma

RYUHO OKAWA

timewarner
books

A *Time Warner* Book

First published in Great Britain in 2004
by Time Warner Books

Copyright © Ryuho Okawa 1994

English translation © the Institute for Research in Human Happiness 2004
Original title: Kokoro-no-Chousen

The moral right of the author has been asserted.

A CIP catalogue record for this book
is available from the British Library.

ISBN 0 316 72690 7

Typeset in Bembo by M Rules
Printed and bound in Great Britain by Clays Ltd, St Ives plc

Time Warner Book Group UK
Brettenham House
Lancaster Place
London WC2E 7EN

www.twbg.co.uk

Contents

CHAPTER THREE

The Essence of Meditation

CHAPTER FOUR

Transcendental Wisdom and Forgiving Love

CHAPTER FIVE

The Benefits of an Egoless Perspective

CHAPTER SIX

Practising the Middle Way

CHAPTER SEVEN

Enlightenment and Spiritual Powers

CHAPTER EIGHT

What Is Karma?

Preface

This book will serve as an excellent guide for those of life's 'travellers' who yearn for the mystical world of religion and seek to deepen their understanding of life from a Buddhist perspective. Now that we have entered a spiritual age the Institute for Research in Human Happiness, which I founded, is proving that true religion can be compatible with a highly intellectualised society. In these times, being an ardent reader of this book can be taken as proof of being in this sense a real intellectual.

True religion teaches the potential and the challenges of the mind. Its teachings convey the spirit of the Buddha and the essence of all religions. This book invites you to explore the infinite heights of a wisdom appropriate to our times. When you understand that practising religion is synonymous with being a pioneer of a new era, you will have reached higher ground; from there you will look out over a whole new world. Together let us take on the challenge of the mind.

Ryuho Okawa
President, the Institute for Research in Human Happiness

CHAPTER ONE

The Law of Cause and Effect

1

Two Types of Religion – The Type that Isolates Humans from God, and the Other that Unites Them with God

J would like to talk about the law of cause and effect in a general way, and give an introductory explanation. This law is very important because it is closely connected to the principle of taking responsibility for the self which is something our Institute, the Institute for Research in Human Happiness, places great emphasis on.

Before proceeding to the main topic, I would like to look at the way in which religions are constructed. World religions can be divided into two broad categories. One type can be called 'the religions that isolate humans from God'. In these God and human beings are quite separate from one another and regarded as completely different kinds of beings. Christianity is typical of this sort of religion. It states that while humans have faith in God as the object of worship, they cannot become God, nor does God become human. Although Jesus Christ is said to be the Son of God and to have acted as a bridge, God and human beings are definitely classified as separate from one another. This is the type of religion that isolates humans from God, and having faith in a power outside oneself is based on this thinking.

The other type could be called 'religions that unite God and humans'. In this type of religion, God and human beings can become one. These religions assert that human beings can approach God, and can become God because within they possess the same divine nature. To put it simply, this means that human beings have, in essence, the same nature as God, so even if they can sometimes be deluded or corrupted by the things of this world, even if at times they make mistakes, if they remove these impurities and continue to refine themselves spiritually they can still become one with God and even become as God Himself. Buddhism is typical of this type of religion, and it is often said to be of the type that unites God and humans. In this type of religion, the teachings focus mainly on the power of the self.

When I say that there are two types of religion, those that place their faith in an outside power and those that focus on the power of the self, and that they correspond to religions that isolate humans from God and those that unite humans with God, I do not mean that one of the two is right and the other wrong. Religions that isolate humans from God regard human beings as weak and God as a being of enormous power. The idea is that before a colossal God, human beings are so small that they should be humble, throwing themselves on the mercy of a power outside of themselves so that they might live a better life through correcting their minds and hearts. As, in this type of religion, people become humble, give thanks, pray to God, and intend to live with God's blessing we cannot say it is wrong. This type of religion, however, tends toward the view that human nature is essentially evil. It is inclined to maintain that human beings are basically sinful and that only by the grace of God can there be forgiveness.

In contrast, religions that unite human beings with God are strong in that they affirm humans can themselves approach God. In other words, they are inclined to assert that human nature is essentially good. Because human beings have the same high nature as God, they can approach Him. But living in this three-dimensional world, their essential nature becomes obscured in different ways and for this reason problems arise. So the main focus of spiritual development is learning how to become free from the bondage and delusions of the third dimension.

Both these types of religion demonstrate right thinking, but for my part I attach greater importance to the idea that human beings have been gifted with a wonderful innate nature, which they can develop through their own efforts. The reason I feel this way is that according to religions that place their faith in an outside power, not much development can be expected from humanity. Of course, I can see that human beings are anxious to be delivered out of their present suffering and want to be saved by someone else as quickly as possible, but when this desire has been fulfilled, there is a tendency to stop right there. After they have been saved and given thanks to God, for the time being they become happy and there tends to be no further progress.

In the religions that unite humans with God, on the other hand, there is an infinite path that opens before human beings, a path that leads to boundless progress and development. If we consider that human beings are souls who reincarnate in this three-dimensional world again and again in order to refine themselves, which type of religion will do more good in the end? From this standpoint, which one will lead as many people as possible to the other shore, to true happiness? Compare the type that causes human beings to plead for forgiveness each time they reincarnate, saying 'I am a child of sin. God, please forgive my sins', with the type that causes them to think, 'Each time I am born into this world, I will refine my soul further, and step by step I will aim to achieve a higher level of enlightenment.' All in all, I recommend religions of the type that believe in the power of the self.

Some people have become so corrupt that there seems to be very little possibility of their developing the power within, but deep down even these people still have some faint aspirations to enlightenment. In such cases, a religion that focuses on an outside power can give them the incentive to lead a better life. In Buddhism, this concept of an outside power emerged in what was called the Pure Land Sect.

2

Equality and Fair Judgement – The Basis of Buddhism

As I have just explained, Buddhism is a religion that unites human beings with God. Our Institute, which is based on the spirit of Buddhism, naturally places more emphasis on this style of religion. The basic reason for this is that we uphold the idea that every human being has the same 'Buddha-nature' within.

There is, of course, the issue of the difference between God and Buddha, and this might have to be considered here. (In the last chapter of one of my books, *The Challenge of Religion*, there is a detailed explanation.)[1] To put it simply, what is called 'Buddha' in Buddhism is a being who experienced a human

---

1 Refer to *The Challenge of Religion* (IRH Press, 1993) by Ryuho Okawa.

life on Earth and returned to the other world to live there as a high spirit with divine powers. This means that a being who has been human can become divine, and this is the basis of the type of religion that unites human beings with God.

In order to achieve this union, a human being must undergo a great deal of spiritual discipline in this world, guiding and saving many. Only after someone has done this can he or she return to the other world as a high spirit with exactly the same powers as Buddha. In Japan, there is a widely held idea that when someone dies that person will become a buddha, but this is utterly wrong. The truth is that a human being can only become a buddha after having accomplished a great deal of work so that the person has become worthy of this.

In religions that isolate humans from God, however, a human being can never become God, no matter how much effort is made. God is an entirely separate being for He is the creator of human beings, while human beings are the creatures or beings who were created. In Judeo-Christian religions, you find the idea that human beings were created from clay or dust that was gathered and mixed, or by breathing life into pieces of broken rib.

If there is a clear distinction between the creator and the created, then the created can never become the creator. There is even the allegory that humans attempted to become like the creator by taking forbidden fruit in the Garden of Eden and were driven out of paradise. In short, the fact that Eve was tempted by the serpent in the Garden of Eden and attempted to eat the fruit of the tree of knowledge signifies that humans tried to become omniscient and omnipotent like God. They tried, but in vain. So here we have a clear distinction between God and human beings; when humans attempted to overstep the line dividing them from God, God became angry.

We can see something similar in the story of the Tower of Babel. When human beings built a very high tower and attempted to reach the kingdom of God, or heaven, God became wrathful and the people suffered a great disaster – they could no longer understand one another's words. This tries to show clearly that God and human beings are quite different types of beings.

As you can see from the concept of the universe as a multi-dimensional structure, which I teach, God and human beings are different. They are different because they belong to different dimensions. But they are also similar, because they have the same innate nature. So, in essence, they are the same, but in terms of the degree of evolution, or the amount of spiritual light they emit, they are different. The inner self of every human being is like a diamond, but how much care it receives and how much it shines like a diamond depends upon the individual. Just as diamonds are graded, depending on the way they refine their souls people naturally settle in different dimensions in the other world, beginning in the fourth dimension, through the fifth, sixth, seventh and eighth to the ninth dimension.

The dimension the soul goes to in the other world corresponds precisely to the level of enlightenment in this world.

Someone who emits a great spiritual light in this world will return to the corresponding world in the beyond. A person who has attained a seventh-dimension level of enlightenment in this world will return to the world in the seventh dimension, and someone with a five-dimensional enlightenment will return to the world in the fifth dimension. So, how much a soul shines in this world corresponds exactly to where it will go in the other world. This is the Buddhist idea.

Accordingly, we can view human beings as having the innate potential to evolve, and in this respect everyone is equal. However, in the process of numerous reincarnations over a long period of time, substantial differences have occurred between souls. It is fair to judge the outcome of a life, as some souls have evolved and others have not. However, all have the potential to evolve, in any era, even now, and when this latent potential comes into contact with the Dharma (Buddhist teachings), which act as a catalyst, it becomes apparent and shines forth. Then there is the opportunity for a great increase in the level of enlightenment and this idea is the core of the spiritual refinement that I teach.

3

Cause and Effect as the Law of the Universe

Now let's look in detail at the main topic: the idea of cause and effect. This idea is that everything has a cause and an effect, and that the world unfolds itself by means of such chains of cause and effect.

Let me give you an example. When molecules of hydrogen and oxygen are heated a chemical reaction occurs resulting in small drops of water. When a large quantity of these drops is collected, water is produced. When a large amount of water is collected, a pond, a river, or an ocean forms. An ocean provides an environment which gives rise to marine life and allows sea creatures to live. When sea creatures live in an area, it then becomes possible for other forms of life to exist by feeding on them. Or take minerals, for instance. They are made up of crystals that are formed through chemical reactions. Plants also require certain conditions to grow; first of all, of course, there must be a seed, and then there needs to be certain nutrients in the soil. When rain falls and the sun shines, plants grow quickly. Around them are herbivorous animals that feed on them; human beings and other creatures also live on them.

First there is the cause, or the combining of one element with another, which gives rise to a new result; this result, in turn, becomes the cause that produces another new result. When we view the world in this way, we see that everything is produced by chains of cause and effect.

For humans, the same idea holds true. First, there is a mother and a father, then a child is born. That child then marries the child of another family and a new child is born. In this way, long uninterrupted family lineages have allowed human history to continue for more than tens of thousands of years. Without such chains of cause and effect, human beings would not exist today. The teachings of Gautama Siddhartha (*Shakyamuni Buddha*), too, have been passed down to us at this time through some two thousand five hundred years simply because humankind has continued to this day.* If humankind had ceased to exist in the time of *Shakyamuni*, his teachings would not have remained. Everything works in this way.

---

* Gautama Siddhartha (Gotama Siddhatta) is the personal name of 'the Buddha' who lived in India in the 6th century BC. He is also called *Shakyamuni* (Sakyamuni) *Buddha*, because he was the Honorable from Sakyas clan.

Here we become aware of an interesting fact. The world is formed according to the law of cause and effect, or the law of causality, and human beings are able to improve themselves and become higher beings depending on the choices they make within the circumstances of this world while undergoing spiritual refinement. As they advance, they are led along the path to Buddha.

In fact, the idea of cause and effect is exactly the same as the law of the universe. In other words, the universe operates under one law or one rule. Everything unfolds itself according to that law. This Earth and all the other stars, nebulae and solar systems are subject to this one law. In three-dimensional space, all things operate according to the law of causality.

As mentioned earlier, there are also chains of cause and effect in the vertical flow of time. There are chains of parents and children, children and grandchildren, grandchildren and great-grandchildren. Plants, too, bear fruit each year and this, in turn, generates the next link in the chain of life. In autumn there is the harvest. At that time, the seeds fall to the ground, or are sown by human hand, and the following year they begin to grow. Again, they bear fruit in autumn and again seeds fall. Similarly, the leaves on the trees bud in spring, grow thick in summer, turn red in autumn and finally they shrivel and fall in winter.

Spatially and temporally, all things arise out of chains of cause and effect. These chains do not exist independently of one another, but are intertwined in complicated ways existing in space and time in this world. That is what is meant by the idea that this world is created by the law of cause and effect.

4

The Power of Reason that Underlies the Law of Causality

The law of causality is the law of the universe; this is what Buddha considers to be the law, so it can also be regarded as Buddha's ideal, the will of Buddha, or even the life of Buddha.* Buddha is the law and the world is created based on this law.

In Christianity, there is a clear distinction between the one who created and what was created. In Buddhism, however, this figurative explanation of the creation of the world is replaced by the idea that everything operates under one law. This law could be termed 'the will of Buddha', 'the ideal of Buddha' or 'the power of Buddha'. In other words, this

---

* Buddha means the Primordial Buddha, which is equivalent to the Creator.

universe was created based on a single law, that is Buddha's will. All things and all phenomena, including human beings, are subject to this law. The law is Buddha.

Shakyamuni Buddha said, 'Those who see the chains of cause and effect see Dharma, and those who see Dharma clearly see how everything unfolds through cause and effect.' So Dharma is the law of causality. The word 'Dharma' has several meanings. First, it refers to 'the teachings'. The law of the universe, or Buddha's Dharma is, in fact, what teaches us to see cause and effect, so if you can fully understand causality, you will understand Dharma. Another meaning of Dharma is 'the whole of creation'. So, those who see Dharma will discover the law of cause and effect operating in all living things, through all the phenomena of this universe.

As I said before, this means that there is nothing in this world that exists that does not have a cause. Look at everyday items such as your clothes, your desk and your watch. First came the raw materials, then before the end product came into existence, the raw materials were processed by human hand. First was an intention to make them, then they were created. All the things of this world are formed by chains of cause and effect. Many things come into existence by means of the human hand. Everything exists through cause and effect, and how and why something exists can be explained in terms of these chains.

What *Shakyamuni Buddha* taught is that Dharma, both the meaning of the teachings and of existence, is also based on the chains of cause and effect, but if we explain only the origin of three-dimensional matter using the idea of causality, there is the possibility that Buddhist ideas will be mistaken for materialistic views. We should be very careful to guard against this.

The explanation for the existence of all things through cause and effect also implies that, for one thing, there is a logical way to see everything, a rational way in which to interpret them. In other words, the explanation itself is a manifestation of the vast power of reason that *Shakyamuni Buddha* embodied. The power of reason, which has had a great influence on certain fields of academic study, such as medicine and the natural sciences, is also inherent in Buddhism. Buddhism is therefore quite different from those religions that merely promise their followers certain benefits, or the dubious new religions so prevalent today. In Buddhism, there is a very rational and logical way of thinking, a scientific approach. If you understand the idea of cause and effect, you will see this clearly.

5

Applying the Idea of Causality to Spiritual Refinement – The Principle of Self-Responsibility

I have just stated that the existence of all things can be explained by the idea of cause and effect. I also said that Dharma, when it is interpreted as the teachings, can mean cause and effect, and vice versa. Simply put, the teachings are what explain the chains of cause and effect. What does this mean?

In reality, human beings are surrounded by two worlds, this three-dimensional world and the 'other' world. This latter is also called 'the Real World', and is the original home of human beings. Occasionally we reincarnate into this world to undergo spiritual refinement, and then we return to the other world. In the process of repeated incarnations, we learn that our lives are subject to the law of cause and effect. No one can escape this law. What we reap depends on how we have tended the seeds we have sown. The seeds are the 'causes', how they have been tended are the 'conditions'. What we reap are the 'effects'.

People are born, grow up in different sets of conditions and, as a result of the way they live, they return to different places in the other world. Some people even go to the realm known as hell that exists in the four-dimensional world. There are innumerable kinds of places in the realm of hell, in fact there are as many hells as there are nightmares that human beings can have.* In the course of your life, you may have had a number of nightmares, but there are actually many, many more kinds of hell than the number of bad dreams you have had, more than the total number of all your classmates' bad dreams put together, so there are not just one or two hundred hells, but thousands and tens of thousands. There are as many realms in hell as there are wrong ways of thinking. If a person's way of thinking is wrong, and it is a thinking no one else shares, a person can create a hell of their own. If the same sort of people gather, they create their own shared hell. Everything is subject to this rule.

In the Buddhist world view, there is no fearsome God who drives people to hell as a punishment or takes others

---

* The universe is multi-dimensional and the world we inhabit is the third dimension which consists of three elements – length, breadth, and height. While heaven stretches from the fourth to the ninth dimensions, hell only occupies a tiny section of the fourth dimension. Those in hell have the chance to return to heaven through self-reflection and repentence.

up to heaven. Instead, everything is determined by this single law. It is true that the law of the soul exists and it is clear what kinds of experiences will cause it to go toward darkness.

Through the decades of a person's present lifetime under this law a person makes choices, exercising free will. Human beings are given complete freedom in their choices. As long as we are human and live on Earth, we cannot survive without certain basic necessities and we have relationships with other people, but within these parameters, we are able to think and act freely. For example, anyone can kill a person if they want to. Although it is possible, people do not actually do this because they restrain themselves with thoughts such as, 'I should not do this'. They may not know the reason why they refrain, but at least they know that such acts ought not be done, or that if they do them it will cause something dreadful to happen. This is because people have a knowledge of good and evil, learned over the course of numerous reincarnations, and this knowledge has penetrated deep into the soul. When they are younger, they may not understand so well what to do, but as they learn from others and from books, they become able to behave correctly. This is because a considerable amount of knowledge is in fact already accumulated in their souls. When something outside of them brings it to their attention, this knowledge is awakened.

If, on the other hand, human beings were born by accident, like flies that just appear by the pond on a sunny day, each time they were born they would have to decide all over again what good and evil are, otherwise there would be no way of dealing with situations. What is good and what is evil in a particular life would have to be decided each time a person was born. In actual fact, however, human beings already have this knowledge to a certain extent from their experience in past incarnations. They possess about eighty per cent of this knowledge innately, and subsequently acquire the remaining twenty per cent while undergoing spiritual refinement in their present lifetime. They will be held responsible for what they have chosen in this life and also in their next life. This is the idea of causality applied to spiritual development in life; no one can escape this law.

6

The Essence of Buddhism – The Concept of the Law of Causality

The chain of cause and effect can be applied spatially as well as temporally. It is the law that governs the universe and it is one of the core teachings of *Shakyamuni Buddha*. It by no means implies atheism or materialism. *Shakyamuni* discovered this law and lived within the law in the best way possible for a human being, and that is why he continues to exist as the Buddha and is considered the highest spiritual entity.

The original nature of the soul is divine, and if you perceive the law of the universe and lead the best possible life in accordance with the law, you can become a being of high spiritual level; this is the core teaching of Buddhism. So when the Buddha appeared, representing the highest human ideals, traditional gods could no longer be regarded as beings of an even higher order. The truth is that the traditional gods are high spirits who incarnated on Earth in times past, but the Buddha emerges as a being surpassing them.

Even the Buddha cannot alter the law of the universe. He embodies this law and manifests it at the highest level. Furthermore, in Buddhism, it is said that anyone can become a buddha through continual spiritual refinement, though it may take many, many years to achieve. Here you can see how marvellous Buddhism is. The Dharma gate is open to everyone.

However, it is essential to know that the results of your life will be judged precisely. Some people say, 'If you believe in such and such, you will be saved', but this sort of simple-mindedness has nothing to do with Buddhism. It is a long way from the essence of Buddhism. For instance, some say that if you chant the name of Amida Buddha or if you worship an image of the Buddha or a particular hanging scroll, you will be saved. They say if you just sit in meditation, you will be saved, or that a mandala will produce happiness. Today, there are numerous sects that call themselves Buddhist, but their teachings are a long way from the true teachings of the Buddha.

The Buddha's actual teaching can be summed up in the following way: 'All things arise through chains of cause and effect. Perceive the chain, and endeavour to improve it. If you do this, you can save yourself. Who is this who can save himself? He is God.' This means that God and human beings are not separated into one who saves and the ones who are saved, but that humans can actually save themselves, which is synonymous with achieving divinity.

So human beings can become divine. By learning and mastering the law we can save both ourselves and others; in other words, we can become high spirits. This is the great difference between Buddhism and religions that isolate humans from God. There are other more profound ideas about the law of causality, but for now if you can understand this much, I will be happy.

CHAPTER TWO

What Is
Buddha-Nature?

1

The Potential for Attaining Enlightenment and Standards for Becoming a Buddha

I would like to discuss the subject of Buddha-nature, which literally means the nature of Buddha. It can also be explained as the nature that enables a person to attain enlightenment. What made *Shakyamuni* a buddha was that he was able to attain enlightenment and he did actually achieve enlightenment. The word 'buddha' means 'enlightened one'. If everyone has Buddha-nature within, it means that every person possesses a nature that will lead them to enlightenment. This can be described in another way as 'the potential for enlightenment'.

However, I would like to remind you of one thing: the potential for enlightenment is simply a potential, it is not the same as a result. This is a very important point to remember. The fact that every individual has the potential to become a buddha, and has a nature that leads to enlightenment, does not necessarily mean that everyone will become a buddha. It is worth noting that to reach the final goal, you have to go through a specific process.

All over the world, religions of all sorts are being practised. As I observe this, one thing that concerns me is that many of the new religions are strange and outlandish and ignorant of the law of cause and effect. I find it troubling because, in many cases, they force people to do peculiar things without explaining logically how doing these things will lead to enlightenment. Meanwhile, many of the traditional religions have become fossilised or degenerated into forms that are now corrupt. Whether the religions are newly established or traditional, the problem they have in common is that they misunderstand the concept of 'Buddha-nature'. What I really mean is that they take enlightenment to be something that can be easily attained. In other words, it seems there is a general tendency to discount the original idea that to attain buddhahood everyone must make an effort. These religions lower the standards for becoming a buddha by promising anyone can achieve this with no effort.

Consider the analogy of human beings who can sail across an ocean to reach what lies beyond. They have the potential to sail vast oceans such as the Pacific or the Atlantic and reach a land beyond. However, if this idea does not persuade anyone to set sail and the ocean is then redefined as something more manageable, we reach a point where we are saying that crossing the ocean is the same as jumping over a puddle – and any human being can jump a puddle in a single leap. But of course the original spirit has been lost completely and it becomes impossible to understand what was originally meant. Was the original aim of the training to jump puddles? Was that what spiritual development was for? Is that what enlightenment is all about?

For a small insect like a beetle, crossing a puddle is a major achievement. But for a human being is there any great achievement in simply stepping over a puddle that has formed on a country road after rain? Does it give the person any sense of accomplishment or joy? Does it give the person the opportunity to develop? The answer is no.

Let us take the example of a person about to cross the Pacific Ocean in a yacht. During the voyage, he will inevitably encounter great adversities. The sun may beat down; there may be rain. He may run out of food or water. His muscles may ache and, exposed to the sun, he may gradually become sunburned. But amid the severe hardships of an attempted ocean crossing, his soul is being strengthened. He is being refined. His thoughts may be deepened by his confrontation with the vastness of the ocean.

He goes through an experience that no one else has had, and he may try to tell others what a wonderful experience sailing the ocean can be. Moved by his story, seeing they too could cross an ocean, others may start out, first practising rowing or sailing their boats in the bay. But what if, several hundred years after his death, crossing an ocean has been mistakenly considered to be the equivalent of crossing a puddle with a single stride? How would the person who had originally sailed across the Pacific Ocean and told others of this wonderful experience feel? Undoubtedly, he would protest that he never said it was as easy as jumping a puddle.

2

Returning to the Original Teachings of the Buddha

If *Shakyamuni* were to see what is happening to Buddhism now in some parts of the world, he would inevitably feel exactly like the man in this story who had crossed the ocean. For forty-five years he taught people how to strengthen their souls and attain a higher state of mind. But now the content of *Shakyamuni*'s teachings and the process of spiritual refinement he described have been lost and ideas of easy salvation dominate, for example, 'If you just do such and such, you will be saved.' I find this state of affairs deeply regrettable.

Some religions instruct people to do certain things, for instance, to pray to Amida Buddha or to worship Kannon (the goddess of mercy) or to chant some Sutras. You have only to do things like burn incense, put your hands together in prayer, or recite the Lotus Sutra for your ancestors. Some people say, 'Tell me, in a word, what does the Institute for Research in Human Happiness require me to do?' When they do not get a clear-cut answer, they criticise the Institute, and say, 'It's a strange religion', 'It's not a religion at all', 'The doctrine is not clear', and so on. However, I would like to say that people who say these sorts of things misunderstand.

Taking into consideration the fact that individuals have different tendencies, *Shakyamuni Buddha* gave different teachings for different individuals so that anyone could attain enlightenment. These teachings were later compiled as the sutras by his disciples. There are said to be eighty-four thousand Sutras, an almost inexhaustible abundance. In terms of sheer quantity, Buddhism has hundreds, even thousands of times more teachings than the other major religions and the teachings are very profound. All these different teachings have their origins solely in the Buddha's intention to bring every single person living on this Earth across to the other shore of enlightenment.

However, many people living now are unable to understand what the soul is. Unable to grasp this concept, some imagine it is a function of the nervous system while others think the soul exists in the brain. Or people think that the soul is the chemical or electrical processes that respond to stimuli and that human beings are, after all, machines that function like computers. As a result they begin to see the Buddha's teachings on the soul and the spirit world as empty, abstract theories, or even as fables and metaphors.

This is perhaps a consequence of the materialism and excessive rationalism that have prevailed from certain philosophical teachings. So we have to return to the Buddha's original teachings and study again with humility what they teach us.

3

How to Gain Complete Understanding of the Inner World

The inner world is invisible. However, you must not think that just because you cannot see the invisible world it does not exist. The invisible world is the very essence of a human being. It is wrong to try and prove its existence by conducting certain kinds of experiments of chemical reactions. The inner world definitely does exist and accepting this completely is the first step to enlightenment.

Although invisible to our eyes and impossible to touch with our hands, the soul does exist in every human being. You possess a soul and others also possess one. If you observe deeply, you will know that the soul also exists in animals and plants, although the spiritual level of these souls may be lower. To be aware of the existence of the soul is the first step toward enlightenment. If you are unable to understand this, you cannot object to the statement that you are living like a machine.

Although you might think the soul is a difficult concept to understand, I would like you to ask yourself once again: 'Human beings can feel happiness. How is this possible?' Children become happy when they eat something delicious, or when parents or teachers praise them. Why is it that they become happy? You too may feel happy when you eat something delicious. Do you think that this is because you are a machine with a nervous system that generates happiness when there is some input? Of course, some sort of chemical reaction may be involved in the process. But have you ever seen a machine that becomes happy? Have you ever heard of a cog getting excited when it was oiled? Or of a car that smiled when its tank was full of fuel? I'm sure you have not. People, however, feel happy. Why is this?

The reason is that we have an awareness that is able to recognise the fulfilment of our wishes and feel happiness. People who do not recognise this are the equivalent of machines. When it is oiled, a machine may work more smoothly but it cannot feel anything. You should realise that to have the ability to feel is quite wonderful. To be able to feel means that there is something within you that feels.

It is said in Buddhism that human beings possess six sense organs – the eyes, the ears, the nose, the tongue, the tactile body and the mind, and six senses: sight, hearing, smell, taste, touch and consciousness. On the basis of these neurological responses we make intellectual judgements. For instance, you feel happy when you eat something delicious; this is a phenomenon caused by the sense of taste. It is your sense of taste that transmits the deliciousness. The reason the sense of taste is transmitting this response is that there is some other part it can transmit to. What does it transmit to? Where does it transmit its pleasure, its joy and happiness? There must be something to receive it.

There is a part of us that receives the sensations and makes judgements about them. The same tongue can experience sweetness when licking something sweet, sourness when licking something sour, a salty taste when it is in contact with something salty and acute pain if it touches something hot and is burned. This means that there is some part of us that sends out these sensations and another part that receives them. In a word, the soul is what receives them. This explanation of the sense of taste is fairly easy to understand.

Let me give you another example. When parents or teachers praise a child, the child experiences happiness. This involves a higher level of perception. In this case, the sense of hearing is involved, which you could say is simply the vibration of the eardrum. However, it is difficult to determine how the vibrating of the eardrum makes a child feel happy. Is it the way that the eardrum vibrates that determines whether or not the child experiences happiness? Imagine, for instance, a robust male teacher who says in a loud voice, 'Hey! You got full marks! Congratulations!' and his voice is so loud that the glass in the window almost shatters. In this situation, the eardrums feel such a strong vibration they might start to ache. The pain may well cause discomfort, but on hearing the loud voice booming, 'You got full marks in the exam', the child would not feel discomfort but rather happiness. If, on the other hand, the teacher is a gentle female, who says in a soft voice, 'Well, dear, you've done very well. You got full marks!' on hearing this the child would also feel happiness. In this situation, the vibrating of the eardrums would be completely different from when the male teacher offered his congratulations. This time, the vibration would be like a breeze. No matter whether the sound is like a strong, gusty wind or a soft, gentle breeze, if you are receiving praise, it is pleasant.

However, if you are being told off in a loud voice, you feel intimidated and fearful. Similarly, if someone makes an offensive remark, a low voice can be upsetting; it may even reduce you to tears. This means that it is not simply the physical vibration that makes you feel happy. Although musical sounds may seem to you to be physical, it is the consciousness deep within you that actually enjoys the music, after the vibrations have passed through the eardrums and brain. If human beings were just machines, they would not notice very much difference between the noise of buckets and the sound of drums. But human beings have a soul that receives information through the six senses and judges whether or not the information is pleasing to them.

4

The Principles of the Soul, the Entity that Makes Judgements

Through my spiritual abilities, I have found that it is not only human beings living on Earth in a physical body who have perceptual senses. Spirits in the other world no longer have physical bodies so they do not have the six sense organs of the body, but they still have exactly the same feelings as they used to have when they were living in this world.

Although spirits do not have ears, they can hear the voices of those who are living in this world. Though they have no eardrums, they can listen to music. If a piece of music they loved when they were living on Earth is being played, they can enjoy it even after they have become spirits. Conversely, they do not enjoy the music which they previously disliked. So spirits retain the same ability to feel even after they have lost their physical bodies. The entity that experiences these feelings is called 'the soul'.

The soul has, of course, an intellectual function that is very much connected to the brain. Some people have good brains while others have duller ones. It used to be said that the brain of a bright person had more folds in it than the brain of someone who was slower. In reality, however, even if the physical body and brain have been lost, a thinking function exists in the soul. In Western medicine, a person suffering from anencephaly, or the congenital absence of a brain, was sometimes treated as less than human. This, however, is a big mistake because humans do not think with their brain; the part of them that does the thinking lies beyond the brain. The brain is rather like a computer, a calculator or a word processor – a machine that processes information. If this machine breaks down, a person's physical body will have difficulty dealing with information, but the soul still receives information accurately.

So the part of us that receives information about the various experiences of this world and makes judgements about whether they are good or bad, beautiful or ugly, pleasant or unpleasant, is the soul. What makes human beings human is the soul, otherwise people would be nothing more than objects moving haphazardly on Earth. Because we have a soul we are human and we are of worth.

Strangely enough, the soul functions according to the same principles in different people, although they have been born to different parents. The sense of good and bad, the sense of beauty and ugliness – these are fairly universal.

Although each person attaches different meanings to things and makes different judgements about them, essentially common to everyone is a sense of beauty when looking at something beautiful, or a sense of sweetness when we eat something sugary. Although people do not share the same parents, a person in one country and someone living on the other side of the world experience the same sense of sweetness when they eat something sweet. For generation after generation, for thousands or even tens of thousands of years, though these families have lived in completely different places, yet they have the sense of the sweetness or the spiciness of food in common. Why is this?

People laugh when they are happy and cry when they are sad. Why? Similar situations may make them angry. Although there may be small variations from person to person, under certain conditions we react in the same way. Although our languages may differ, there are universal principles of the soul common to all people.

5

How the Buddha-Nature Manifests

This is in fact how the Buddha-nature in our souls manifests. What is Buddha-nature? There are certain ways of feeling and experiencing the different events that occur in this world. This is the beginning of Buddha-nature. In a dark world, everyone senses the darkness, and in a bright world people sense the brightness. If you become happy, you feel joy. The fact that everyone shares similar ways of feeling is evidence that everyone has Buddha-nature.

Buddha-nature, the nature of enlightenment, actually means that every person has the potential to make certain value judgements as a faculty of the soul. If you are alone, you feel and think in a certain way. You make judgements, saying to yourself, 'If it goes this way, I will feel happy; if it goes another way, I will feel unhappy.' If human beings had perfect freedom to do everything in their own way, everyone would go in the direction that delighted them and made them happy. However, in reality, you live on Earth with many other people, with animals and plants, so a new consideration arises, of whether or not your happiness leads to the happiness of others. If you were alone, you would have complete freedom, but there is actually another consideration – the happiness to be found in relationships with others.

Suppose you are married and have a family, what makes you happy? Every morning, you go to the office and after working hard from morning to night, sometimes getting told off by your boss, you come home tired. There may be times when you must do things you do not want to do in order to achieve success at work. If you repeat this day in and day out, at times you may feel you do not want to go to work and that you would rather just stay at home and sleep. This might be your happiness. However, you have a spouse and children to support. A financial base is essential to establish a husband–wife relationship and a family. In order to secure a financial base, you have to produce something of value by doing work that is valuable to society and, in return, you can earn money. Your salary takes care of the day-to-day expenses of living and the costs of bringing up the children, so you find yourself in a situation where you must go to work, even if it is unpleasant to you.

This judgement is totally different from the natural feelings of like and dislike. You go to work every day out of a higher-level necessity, suppressing your own feelings of like and dislike. You commute to work every day. If you are thinking in terms of like and dislike, for example, of the physical discomforts of fatigue, feeling hot and sweaty, or being cramped and having aching legs, you would move in the direction of avoiding these situations. However, for the sake of a higher level of happiness – to protect your family, to prepare for the future and to create a happy home – you endure these hardships.

If a person lives alone, he can live with more freedom. However, when his goal is to share his happiness with others in the framework of relationships, he tries to limit a part of his freedom in favour of the good of the whole society. He tries to create harmony with others to bring about the progress and development of the whole. Therefore, people put certain limits on their instincts which involves some sort of self-sacrifice and people act in ways that create higher levels of happiness.

To put it simply, at a very primitive level, our Buddha-nature initially finds expression in basic emotions such as pleasure and pain, happiness and anger, like and dislike. At the next stage, where people coexist with others in communities, the individual will inevitably be in situations where basic feelings and preferences have to be restrained to create a higher order of happiness. In such situations, the ability to make right choices is a higher manifestation of our Buddha-nature.

In making such choices there is a rule: human beings will be happy if they make a certain kind of choice in a certain kind of situation. For instance, hitting someone in a boxing match is different from hitting a person in an ordinary fight. Hitting a person in a fight makes both parties unhappy whereas in a boxing match it is done within certain rules. In the process, boxers develop their muscles and, whether they win or lose, they find a higher level of happiness in making the effort to strive for a particular goal.

Human beings have created a number of values that are not visible on this Earth. These invisible values lead us to strive in the direction of the happiness of the whole of humanity through endeavouring to take control of our free will for a higher purpose. This is what Buddha-nature, or the nature of enlightenment, is all about.

6

Aspiring to Realise Buddha's Ideal

On this Earth, humans exist first and foremost as individual selves. Since each individual originates from Buddha's light, to attain happiness it is required that the self should exert its own particular quality fully. On the other hand, human beings do not live alone but hand in hand with others, so this requires that they live for the common happiness. How do we balance these two kinds of happiness, the happiness of the individual and the happiness of the whole?

Throughout history, religion, philosophy and morality were in fact created to answer this question. Their original purpose was to generate principles which would enable many people to live happily together. Religion in particular created these principles from the perspective of

God or Buddha. Philosophy considered them in a more intellectual and rational way. Morality attempted to consider them as rules of everyday living. Religion also concentrated on a happiness that would be valid both in this world and the other. This is how religion came into being.

All living things in this world, including plant life, are seeking their own happiness, and at the same time they need to contribute to the happiness of others. If there is a conflict of interests in these two directions, then efforts must be made to bring them into harmony. This is Buddha's ideal. The part of us affirming that Buddha's ideal is valuable and wonderful is called Buddha-nature. It is the aspiration and the willingness to respond to Buddha's ideal. This is what Buddha-nature is.

In short, those who have abandoned this way of thinking and live in a quite opposite way, who shamelessly abuse or denounce Buddha's ideal, are considered to have 'sold their souls to the devil'. However, this does not mean they did not originally have a Buddha-nature. They are going against their Buddha-nature simply because they are misguided or because there is a veil of delusion that covers their eyes preventing them from seeing.

So Buddha-nature is within every individual. Buddha-nature is the part of you which aims to realise Buddha's ideal. What is this ideal? It is that every individual is able to live fully at the highest level giving out a brilliant light and, at the same time, able to bring their life into harmony with the ideals of society and work for the advancement of these ideals. In this chapter, I have dealt with the question 'What is Buddha-nature?' in relation to general issues. I hope this will guide you toward enlightenment.

CHAPTER THREE

The Essence
of Meditation

1

The Purpose of Meditation

I would like to explore the meaning of meditation in some depth. On hearing the word meditation perhaps you are reminded of Zen meditation (Zazen, sitting in a cross-legged posture) or yoga. It is true that Zen meditation and yoga are ways to practise meditation but regrettably many people seem to think of meditation as simply sitting without thinking or sitting in a particular posture.

Why do people practise meditation in the first place? Many people do not seem to have ever considered this very deeply; they seem conscious only of the form or style. However, we need to go to the roots. What I am saying is that we need to think once again about the true purpose of meditation.

The Japanese Zen master Dogen (1200–1253 CE) introduced a style of meditation called 'Shikantaza', which means 'just sitting without a purpose', simply sitting quietly. He was the founder of one of the major schools of Zen, and this method of meditation has long been accepted as an important part of Zen training. In yoga too, which originated in India, there are many styles of meditation but it appears some of these are directed only at maintaining health or as physical disciplines. Although yoga is certainly a method of meditation that has been handed down through the ages, I have the impression that those who practise it are seeking the essence of meditation in the three-dimensional world.

Where did meditation originate? Meditation itself is, of course, not the invention of Gautama Siddhartha, *Shakyamuni Buddha*. In India it was a traditional practice long before *Shakyamuni* lived, and in religions other than Buddhism it was a method of developing mental concentration. It is true that meditation has always been associated with religion.

What is the purpose of meditation? It is actually a method of communicating with the heavenly world or the world of high spirits. Those who do not understand this may practise meditation for health, or perhaps they simply think it is good to spend time just sitting without thinking about anything, without a purpose. However, we are not trees or stones. If it was only a matter of sitting still, trees and stones could do this much better than humans. But we have hearts and minds and this is the essence of being human.

The three-dimensional world where we lead our daily lives is filled with coarse thought vibrations and many of these third-dimension thoughts are quite negative. In daily life, sometimes your mind becomes disturbed, for example, when you hear shocking news or after arguing with someone. When you hear sad news, your mind may waver; drinking and singing in a bar, you may lose control. So sometimes you must isolate yourself from all these daily activities, leave the vibrations of the third dimension behind and ask what your true self is. The act of discovering your true self is the purpose of meditation.

2

Refining the Vibrations of the Mind

Although the basic style for meditation is usually sitting cross-legged, you do not have to stick to this form. The first step is to distance yourself from daily life and to do this you need to find a place where you will not be disturbed by worldly vibrations. Avoid noisy places or a room where the telephone might ring or a room where people often go in and out. Choose a quiet place where you will not be interrupted for a time so that you can concentrate on your dialogue with yourself.

After shutting out the outside world, the waves of your mind will gradually change, becoming calmer and calmer until your thoughts are no longer attuned to the wavelengths of three-dimensional thought. Once you enter this state, which is quite different from the everyday, your mind will no longer waver and thoughts about various people and everyday matters will also gradually disappear. You will begin to experience a feeling of relaxation as if you were somewhere in a village deep in the mountains or lying on a beach relaxing all day long. This is the first stage of meditation practice.

To escape the vibrations of the third dimension and discover your true self it is necessary that the physical body be relaxed. Choose the posture that is the most comfortable for you. Although in India the traditional style of sitting meditation is a cross-legged posture, you do not necessarily have to keep to this. This posture is fine for people who are accustomed to it, but for most modern people, sitting in this way can be a distraction for the mind because they are continually having to check their posture. Remember that what you have to do now is relax the body and calm the mind.

When you are relaxed, gradually regulate your breathing – inhale and exhale deeply from the abdomen, repeat this deep breathing slowly and rhythmically so that oxygen circulates through the body easily and the heart settles down. The brain waves also become more subtle, calmer, so your mind is freed from the concerns of everyday life.

This breathing has another good effect on the physical body. As you control your breathing, oxygen-rich blood circulates through the body, helping to remove any congestion of blood in the brain. When you come under negative spiritual influences you are usually affected in the parts of the body where blood has become congested, or where there is a lot of fatigue, for instance, at the back of the head, the neck, shoulders and the lower back. Parts which become stiff easily are in fact points where stray spirits can attach themselves to a person. These spirits respond to the wavelengths of inharmonious vibrations from the physical body and when the two correspond with one another, possession can often occur.

So first of all, it is very important to regulate and calm the rhythms of the physical body. Those who are constantly possessed or easily fall under the control of stray spirits must be especially careful of this. Those who are easily exhausted by going out or who feel very heavy and tired in crowded places are vulnerable to possession. Breathe in and take in fresh oxygen, imagining that you are allowing the blood to circulate throughout your entire body, from your head to your neck, your shoulders and your back. This will eliminate all inharmonious vibrations from the body.

In fact, to remove less serious possession it is best to begin by regulating the physical body. When you are very tired there is usually a congestion of blood in some part of the body, so light aerobic exercise will help improve the circulation of blood and allow you to receive more light. After exercising, relax your body and regulate your breathing. By letting go of the worldly vibrations of the concerns of the third dimension your mind will be on a calmer wavelength, and as you feel calmer, feelings of joy and happiness will gradually well up. This feeling of happiness is proof that you are regaining your original self, though you may still only sense this rather vaguely. Without refining the vibrations of the mind, it is extremely difficult to communicate with the Real World.

3

Surface Consciousness and the Subconscious

If you become absorbed in mental concentration without calming the vibrations of your mind, this will allow possession by stray spirits. Some people can actually receive negative spiritual influences to a great extent. Before entering a meditative state, you should always keep your mind serene. If you practise concentration while you are still very angry or filled with complaints and discontent, stray or malicious spirits can easily enter.

Because we live in the three-dimensional world and are usually concerned only with physical matters, our minds are easily contaminated by the wavelengths of the third dimension. This is both good and bad. The advantage is that if we are exclusively tuned to the wavelengths of the third dimension, stray spirits will have a difficult time possessing us.

Actually, it is hard for stray spirits to keep up with people who work busily every day. At the same time, however, the disadvantage of a busy life is the fact that if we are always busy, it is extremely difficult for high spirits to contact and inspire us. In a meditative state, we are subject to both positive and negative spiritual influences.

We often come across the terms 'surface consciousness' and the 'subconscious'. Essentially, before we are able to contact the spirit world, the door to our subconscious needs to be open and for this to happen we have to gradually quiet the surface consciousness. What is surface consciousness? When you are talking with others, doing calculations or paperwork at the office, for example, your brain is working to the full. When the brain is functioning constantly, the surface consciousness is to the fore. On the other hand, when we are relaxed the mental activity connected to the functioning of the brain calms down and the subconscious, which is usually hidden deep within, starts to surface instead. The inner world, a world of pure images, which you perhaps sometimes experience in dreams, then emerges.

When the door of the subconscious is open, there is the possibility of contacting both heaven and hell. Those who always live in a good-hearted way, who try to have good thoughts and do good deeds can easily start contacting high spirits such as their guardian and guiding spirits as soon as they silence the surface consciousness. But those who have few good thoughts and hardly ever endeavour to do good deeds are very likely to come under negative spiritual influences.

So the method of meditation that I will explain here has much to do with your daily thoughts and actions. People do not always try to correct their state of mind or endeavour to pursue Right Mind. Although some may have studied the concept of right and wrong in philosophy classes at one time, in the course of daily life they have probably never thought deeply about it. Someone who constantly checks on his or her thoughts to see whether they are right or wrong can be said to have a religious disposition. Usually, people do not have a habit of checking their state of mind or saying to themselves, 'I've just had a wrong thought' or 'I've just had a good thought'. They are not normally in the habit of examining each of their actions, thinking 'I did the right thing' or 'I did something wrong'.

But as you become more spiritual and contemplative through studying the Truth you will become able to examine your thoughts one by one. 'This is a good thought', 'This is a bad thought' or 'I've just had a wrong thought'. You can also do the same with your actions. If you do this, you are very unlikely to be affected by negative spiritual influences, even in a state of mental concentration.

4

Self-Reflection – Removing the 'Rust' from Your Mind

If you are not usually in the habit of checking your thoughts and deeds but would like to meditate in your spare time, first shut yourself off from the vibrations of the third dimension and calm the waves of your mind. When you feel the door to your subconscious is about to open, remove any 'rust' that has accumulated. If there are rough or uneven parts in your mind, stray spirits can sneak in at these spots. It is as if they can throw a rope and pull themselves up into your mind, so before stepping fully into your subconscious, you need to correct your state of mind, examining your thoughts and deeds one at a time.

What should you examine first? Usually, it is most important to reflect on your day, 'today'. Ask yourself: What was your day like? What kind of thoughts passed through your mind from the time you woke? Were those thoughts right? Did you have any malicious thoughts toward others? Did you think anything negative? Did you do anything wrong? In this way, you can reflect on your thoughts and actions that day.

After you have examined them, decide not to repeat anything you might have done wrong. If you had wrong thoughts toward someone, feel sorry and correct your thoughts. If you have done something wrong, make up your mind never to repeat the same mistake. When you have finished cleaning your mind for that day, extend your range back further, recalling what has happened over the past week. It is not very difficult to recall what has happened within the last week. Examine the week's thoughts and actions thoroughly, checking whether they were right or wrong in the light of the Truth.

When you have done this, you can go back further and examine the last month. How did you do this month? Did you have negative thoughts? Have you made any mistakes? Have you improved yourself in accordance with the Truth? Have you been making sufficient effort? Have you been fulfilling your mission as a disciple of Buddha? Have you accomplished whatever you needed to? How much progress have you made, compared with last month? If you have not made any progress, this means you are wasting the life that has been given to you by Buddha. Are you thankful? Do you feel grateful to be alive? Do you give thanks to Buddha for all that is on this Earth? Are you grateful to others for their help? You should reflect on the last month in this way.

Next, reflect on the year. What were you doing at the same time last year? What have you thought about and done since then? Have you made any progress compared with last year? Have you succeeded in solving your own problems or improving your character? Are your character and your problems getting better or worse? You can reflect on the year in this way. Through this your body and mind will become purer.

If you have plenty of time, reflect on all that has happened since your birth, dividing your life into several periods. For example, ask yourself what kind of child you were from birth to three years old. Project your life onto the screen of your mind as if you were seeing it on a movie screen. You will see your parents, brothers and sisters, uncles, aunts, grandparents, neighbours and all those who were around you. How do you appear in each scene? Then reflect further, up to the time you entered primary school. Reflect on how you appear at primary school. What about junior school and high school? And after that? Reflect on each period, one at a time, recollecting the important turning points in your life, then come back to yourself in the present. By this time, it is very likely that before you have realised it, tears will be welling up in your eyes. As these tears stream down your cheeks, they wash away the impurities of your mind.

5

Reflective Meditation – From Self-Reflection to Meditation

No one asked you or taught you to cry, but as you reflect on your past, quite naturally you will experience feelings of repentance and regret that bring tears. Your tears are the evidence that you have Buddha-nature within you.

There are wicked people in this world and you might say that there are some who are born rogues or villains. But even these people cry when they reflect on past thoughts and actions and realise how foolish they have been. The fact that we all have the ability to reflect on ourselves and become aware of our own foolishness is proof that every single one of us has Buddha-nature. Although there might be differences in the depth of our reflection or in the way we live, there is one rule; deep in our hearts we all know the standards used to judge whether we are right or wrong. When we realise our own errors during self-reflection, we shed tears. Shedding tears is not a function of the brain, nor is it a function of the eyes; it is a result of the strong emotions coming up from the soul. The reason you are so moved is that you have caught a glimpse of your true self.

You should first attune your mind and body to relaxing, then go into reflection and examine your past. By the time you shed tears, your heart is purer. Needless to say, it is not enough to do this just once; you have to repeat this self-reflection over and over from time to time. It is difficult for those of you who have already lived a long time to finish reflecting on the past all at once; you will need to divide your life into several periods and recall them in order. Because it is not easy to remember things that happened a long time ago, I advise you occasionally to set aside time and choose a proper place to reflect more deeply on your past.

Through reflecting on yourself, you can gradually calm your mind and relax your spirit until you go into a state of deep concentration, and this is what we call 'reflective meditation'. This is the method *Shakyamuni Buddha* always used to enter a meditative state. Although it might be quite easy for a religious aspirant to concentrate, without reflective meditation there is a risk of coming under negative spiritual influences. To avoid this sort of danger, you need to practise self-reflection before going deep into the recesses of your mind. This allows you to concentrate safely, without taking any risk.

As you reflect on yourself and enter a meditative state, your mind will become more distinctly separate from this three-dimensional world and you will gradually tap into the treasure house of the subconscious. Your real self is now stepping into the Real World, the world you originally came from. This is the world of meditation.

6

The Essence of Meditation – The Source of Spiritual Energy

A s you enter the state of meditation, your mind is taken out of this three-dimensional world and immersed in a dimension beyond this one – the fourth dimension or higher. If you should die while in a state of meditation, your soul will go to a place in the other world that corresponds exactly to the state of mind you have attained at that time. If your state of mind corresponds to a kind of hell, you will go to hell, and if it corresponds to heaven you will return to the level in the heavenly world that matches it. Strangely enough, there is a certain level in each person's thinking and people cannot harbour lofty ideas that are too different from their usual thinking. Even if you sometimes try to think the very highest thoughts, you have your own limits and it is not easy to go beyond that level.★

When you meditate, your true self returns to the world it originally came from. It is possible for most people to return to heaven, but how high a level of heaven you can ascend to and whether or not you will become a Bodhisattva (angel) is another question. Then there is the question of how high a realm you are allowed to enter in heaven and this has a lot to do with how far you have progressed in refining your soul through your daily endeavours.

Of course, we have disciplined our souls in past lives and through countless incarnations each soul has acquired a certain strength. Actually, it is the capacity of the soul that determines the extent to which the treasure house of the subconscious can be opened. So I would not say that you can achieve everything through spiritual refinement in this lifetime alone, but I will emphasise here that you can at least contact your own guardian spirit as a result of your endeavours in this lifetime by getting rid of the rust and impurities in your mind and through refining the mind. This means everyone can reach the stage of 'Arhat', the state of mind corresponding to the upper realms of the sixth dimension.[2]

★ People with a mental disability may be believed as having no power of thought, but actually the entity that thinks and makes judgements is one's soul, which resides unhurt within them. See page 38 (Ch. 2 Sec. 4)

2 Refer to chapter four of *The Laws of the Sun* (Lantern Books, 2001) and chapter six of *The Essence of Buddha* (Time Warner Books, 2002) by Ryuho Okawa.

If you are always careful to clean your mind and are in the habit of concentrating, naturally you will be able to contact your brother and sister souls and your guardian spirit who reside in the world of your subconscious.[3] This experience will give you a feeling of bliss that is beyond words. You will also feel that warm eyes are always watching over you and you are being supported in your everyday life. You will feel so thankful and warm-hearted that you will want to be good to everyone around you.

Meditation does not exist just for its own sake. By practising meditation, you are given the chance to contact the world from which you originate and you will glimpse images of an ideal world. During meditation, you will receive light from the other world through your brother or sister souls or from more advanced guiding spirits, so you can transform it into a source of vitality and a source of energy for your everyday life. This is the essence of meditation.

Through meditation, you can regularly correct the orbit of your life and acquire a renewed zest for living, which you will be able to use as the power to spread goodness in this world and as a source of spiritual energy. For these reasons, meditation is of tremendous importance. I hope you will once again return to the starting point and think deeply about refining your mind through meditation, using this chapter as your reference.

3 Refer to *The Laws of the Sun*, chapter two, ibid.

CHAPTER FOUR

Transcendental
Wisdom and
Forgiving Love

1

What is
Transcendental Wisdom?

I would like to talk about the term 'transcendental wisdom' (*panna* in Pali or *prajna* in Sanskrit). This phrase is a key to understanding the meaning of enlightenment in Buddhism. As well as an in-depth explanation of transcendental wisdom, I would also like to discuss how this wisdom relates to the stages of love.

Love is generally seen as separate from wisdom, but the different stages of love actually correspond to the various levels of enlightenment and attaining transcendental wisdom is generally said to be synonymous with attaining enlightenment. Why is this? To acquire transcendental wisdom, you need to start by maintaining the correct attitude to spiritual development in your daily life. Simply put, you are required to practise continuously and carefully the 'Three

Essentials of Learning', which are the precepts, meditation and wisdom.

As you continue to control your thoughts and deeds daily according to the precepts, and to meditate and accumulate wisdom, you will eventually experience liberation. As a result, you will attain the state of mind known as nirvana (*nibbana* in Pali). The wisdom you will gain in the state of nirvana is called transcendental wisdom. This is an inexplicably profound and pure wisdom that can be described as crystal clear. Throughout the ages, Buddhist seekers of Truth have yearned for this profound wisdom. They have constantly asked, 'What is the true meaning of attaining transcendental wisdom?' and 'What are the results?' From ancient times, these have been common subjects of inquiry for seekers.

To the question, 'If you attained transcendental wisdom, what would your state of mind be?' the simple answer is that you would see into your being, into the being of others and into the whole world. In other words, while still living in this three-dimensional world, you would understand clearly what kind of world this is and the reason you are being allowed to live now, in relation to other people. To put it in another way, transcendental wisdom brings a deep realisation that you are 'being allowed to live', rather than that you are living proactively.

Intellectual perception (*vinnanna* in Pali and *vijnana* in Sanskrit) is based on the understanding that you are living proactively, or that you yourself are leading an active life and making positive choices for yourself. In contrast, one who has attained transcendental wisdom will embrace a deep sense of being allowed to live. Although an active and positive attitude to life is commendable, there is a higher state of transcendental wisdom – the understanding that you and also others are being allowed to live and that this world exists to allow all of us to live.

There is a notable difference between intellectual perception and transcendental wisdom. Intellect allows us to observe and analyse other people and events that occur in society, but not to see into ourselves. Just as an index finger can point at other people but not at itself, or like a sword that can cut other things but not itself, the intellect allows us to see other people and things in the world analytically, from the fixed standpoint of ego, but it does not allow us to see into ourselves.

When you reach the state of transcendental wisdom, you are detached from the ego and see yourself, others and the things of this world as they truly are. You are keenly aware that you are being allowed to live. You understand that all things in this world, whether they bring joy or sadness, suffering or anxiety, are here to allow you to live your life, that everything in this world exists as material for learning and that this world is valuable as a place to learn. With transcendental wisdom, you understand why the world exists, why you are living here now, how you came to be born and how you will come to leave this world.

The perspective you acquire through intellect is narrower than this; it provides the kind of wisdom that is necessary to make better choices in this world, to improve yourself and become exceptional. Although this wisdom is very important for character building and self-improvement, it still provides only a limited understanding.

As you come to acquire transcendental wisdom, you realise that you have lived through all eternity, reincarnating again and again in this vast universe of which the spirit world is a part, repeating the process of birth, life and death, and returning to the other world. You understand that through these countless incarnations you come to know your own essence and the essence of the lives of others. You realise that you and everyone else are all here together to develop and refine your souls, like students living in the same era. Moreover, you will start to see that although there are sad and painful experiences in this world, they are not actually substantial but occur as experiments in this world of matter, which is a training ground to refine souls.

Transcendental wisdom is an enlightenment in which we realise that all beings are transient and essentially without ego. All things, including the physical body and the phenomena of this world, are transient. Everything changes and transforms constantly. Although things seem to exist around us, all creation is egoless. It does not truly exist, but is simply made to appear for a limited time by the will of the great universe to provide us with a training ground for our souls.

2

Intellectual Perception and Spiritually Nurturing Love

'The stages of love' is one of the most important teachings of our Institute and it explains that love develops in stages.[4] The lowest stage is taking love, which is a form of love that leads in the wrong direction. Next comes instinctive love. Above this is fundamental love, which is the most common form of giving love. Next is spiritually nurturing love, a highly advanced form of giving love. Then comes forgiving love, the love practised by a person who has experienced a deep spiritual awakening.

As I explained earlier, intellectual perception is very close to cognition, but it is centred mainly on the mental function and is related to judgement which is based on the six

---

4   Refer to *The Laws of the Sun*, chapter three, ibid.

senses – sight, hearing, smell, taste, touch and conscious-ness.* A higher level of spiritual functioning may arise from the intellect, but it still represents only a limited functioning of the soul, up to the sixth-dimensional level. Using intel-lect alone, it is not possible to go beyond this level. In order to go beyond and enter the world of the seventh dimension or higher you must attain spiritual awareness and have a deep sense of the spirit world.

While intellectual perception may have some spiritual aspects, it is essentially a mental faculty that can be developed only within this three-dimensional world where we progress through competing with one another and making a clear distinction between the self and others. We can say that the development of love up to the stage of spiritually nurturing love is closely related to acquiring intellectual perception, because to practise spiritually nurturing love in the true sense, the ability to distinguish between good and evil is vital. Unless you are able to distinguish between good and evil, or what is superior from what is inferior, you will never make progress or develop.

If everyone stopped developing at kindergarten level, could society continue to progress? Kindergarten children do not really understand good and evil. Unless the self is firmly established, you cannot tell the difference between good and evil. As you develop on the basis of a firmly established sense of self, you can also help others to grow. Having under-stood the relationship of self to others, and the difference

----

* See page 35 (Ch.2 Sec.3)

between them, people make rules to avoid conflicts. Observing these rules then gives rise to the distinction between right and wrong; following the rules is good and breaking them is bad. These rules indicate the correct way to live which most people accept, and they can be described as the criteria by which people can distinguish between good and evil in this world on Earth.

Trying to observe the rules of this world is very important to achieve spiritual growth. In fact, without this endeavour we cannot refine our souls. In the course of establishing the self, it is extremely important for our spiritual refinement that we study our relationships with others and how we should live in relation to them in this world. As you can see, understanding good and evil and learning the rules for distinguishing between them is a major part of our spiritual training in this world.

3

Looking into the Origins of Good and Evil

When you are able to see things from the standpoint of transcendental wisdom, which as we have said is higher than intellectual perception, you clearly begin to see the origin of the rules of this world and why they came into being. In order to understand this perspective, you need to consider why rules have been necessary.

Let us take an example. There are differences between men and women. Some people may simply recognise that men and women are different. Others may take this a step further and reach the conclusion that it is not good to discriminate between them and that they should be treated as equals. Through studies of the two genders from various perspectives, many rules have been created in this three-dimensional world. However, the question of the relationship between the two genders cannot be answered if one attempts to do this solely on the basis of the values of this world. Without inquiring deeply into the way in which God or Buddha created the world, we cannot understand the reason both men and women exist. When your understanding deepens to the point of seeing the differences in the souls of the two genders rather than differences in physical appearance, you will have fresh insight into the spiritual development of this world.

Another example to use in contemplating the origin of rules is criminal law where we find rules such as 'do not kill other human beings' and 'do not steal'. You may understand these rules purely from a subjective point of view as meaning that you should not do anything you would not like others to do to you. However, from a more profound perspective you will realise that these acts are wrong because they go against the ideal of God or Buddha, His ideal when He created humankind.

When people argue about saving or putting an end to life in the physical body, the conclusion is generally that preserving life is good and killing is evil. Our lives in this world are limited and everyone dies eventually, but when we truly understand that Buddha has entrusted human beings with His ideal of creating utopia on Earth and respect for all life, then our perspective becomes even more profound.

This awareness can also change our views on crime. Good and evil do exist in this three-dimensional world. Good and evil were first defined by philosophy and ethics and in modern society good and bad are prescribed by the law. For those actions not covered by specific laws, common sense provides a standard for determining whether actions are good or bad, and other people are usually offended by what is bad and take action to put a stop to it.

At another level, transcendental wisdom allows you to manifest Buddha-nature, a memory deep in our souls, then to examine whether or not other people's thoughts and actions help this to shine through. But before you reach this state of mind, you of course need to go through a process of learning to recognise good and evil in this world. In order to advance further and reach a standpoint of transcendental wisdom, you need to have the ability to see through to the origin of good and evil. On reaching this level, you will clearly understand the nature of the evil that exists in this world. You will come to see that evil does not really exist in and of itself, but that it arises when people come into conflict with one another, because each wishes to live in their own way.

Evil arises in relation to people, time and place. In other words, evil arises in relations between people when proper timing has been disregarded and when there has been an error of judgement about place or one's position in relationship to others. If you have done something inappropriate to someone, evil can result. There are things you should not do to other people, even if it is not a problem when you do the same to your spouse. There are things you are encouraged to do with your own children but not with the children of others. Likewise, there are things you are allowed to do with business associates but not with others. The situation changes according to whom you are interacting with.

Similarly, the timing of doing something also makes a difference. There are things that you should do early in the morning, things you should do in the middle of the day and things you should do in the evening. For instance, if you are in the habit of sleeping during the day and working in the middle of the night, of course you will have difficulty adapting yourself to society. There are also actions that minors are considered too young for. Those who are under age are prohibited from drinking and smoking because these actions are harmful to them both physically and mentally.

There can also be errors of judgement involving place. While it is acceptable for children to be mischievous at kindergarten, to play a trick on someone in an office will create confusion so it would most likely be considered wrong. Screaming in a crowded train is out of place. So whether a person's actions are good or bad also depends on where they take place. As you can see, distinguishing between good and evil depends on the interaction of people, time and place.

4

Seeing the World from the Perspective of Your Guardian Spirit

As I have said, good and evil arise in relation to people, time and place, and an action is considered good if it works out harmoniously for everyone around it, but is considered evil if it causes disharmony. However, you should give further consideration as to why disharmony or discord occurs until you are able to perceive that they are the result of the ways in which people think and act.

To take this a step further, you should consider how people have developed their own particular way of thinking. Is it the result of wrong knowledge they have acquired or of their home background? Is it the result of their karma from previous lives or a tendency in their thinking? In this way, try and examine each person's way of thinking and the pattern of their actions. What made this particular person do this?

What will the result be of what the person is doing now? If that person continues to live without making any changes, what will happen? As you continue to look at the ways different people behave, as if you were looking at them from the viewpoint of your guardian spirit, this will lead you to see things from a perspective of transcendental wisdom.

You can see yourself and others, your environment, your family, your company or school as your guardian spirit sees them. You can look at each day of your life, your whole life, your relationships with friends and family, your relationship with society and with the times from the perspective of your guardian spirit. Acquiring this perspective is a very important element of spiritual development to attain transcendental wisdom.

In the course of your life, you may have a major quarrel with someone and feel hatred toward that person for many years. You may experience many types of failure or accidents. You may fall ill or suffer an injury. In fact, it is impossible to avoid these sorts of undesirable events. Yet, I would like you always to try to imagine how these events would look to your guardian spirit. Make a habit of reviewing each of your experiences in this way and this will allow you to understand them more deeply, rather than seeing them as simply good or bad, or considering them merely to be problems of like and dislike.

Your guardian spirit knows your life plan and what you intended to accomplish in this lifetime. If you always try to look at yourself from the perspective of your guardian spirit, you will gradually come to understand how your life appears to those eyes. Even if you have taken a wrong turning, you will be able to get clues as to how to reshape your life from this point on.

Let us look at several cases. Some of you may complain about your parents, but just imagine what would have happened to you if both your parents had died immediately after your birth. You might have been adopted or sent to an orphanage. Another example is the man who always complains about his wife, saying he has a hard time because she is so inefficient. But imagine if he had never had the chance to marry anyone? Others complain about their educational background, saying the university they graduated from was not their first choice and because of that they are unhappy. But what if they had not been admitted to any university and so had not been able to get a degree? Yet others complain about an illness, but what sort of life would they have had if they had been born handicapped?

As you can see in these examples, when you examine your present life from a completely different angle, forgetting the past completely and starting out with a clean slate, you can see anew the various problems you are facing. As if rewinding a tape and playing it over and over again, take a fresh look at your own likes and dislikes, what you consider to be good and bad, and at your relationships with the people around you. When you reach this level in looking at things, it means that you have reached a state of transcendental wisdom.

Once you have attained this level, you will be able to stand back and see yourself with detachment. At present, you may complain, 'I don't like that person and maybe he doesn't like me either', 'I'm not on good terms with my friend', 'My colleague and I are angry with each other', 'My wife and I are fed up with each other', or 'My children and I do not really love each other', and so on. However, you can still stop and think, asking yourself calmly what would have happened if you had never had these relationships, if you had had a completely different life. This should lead you to consider the possibility of a completely different understanding of good and evil, and help you to realise that you also have been the cause of other people's unpleasant experiences.

5

Transcendental Wisdom and Forgiving Love

It is now clear that the state of transcendental wisdom is very close to a level of love as high as forgiving love. In the state of forgiving love, you are able to understand deeply the pain and sorrow people face while living in this world.

For spiritual development we live in a physical body.
That is why everyone makes so many mistakes in the
 course of a life.
We cannot avoid making mistakes,
As we feel our way blindly through life.
This is the very nature of living.
In this life, we have to fumble our way through,
So all of us make many mistakes.
But understanding fully that we are living together and

Blindly feeling our way through the darkness of this
  world together,
Let us encourage one another to try not to dwell on
  the evil in others
And also try not to dwell on the good we do for
  others.
Let us all live together in harmony,
Not locking horns,
But as friends sharing an era.

This view of life illustrates a religious viewpoint that is characterised by forgiving love and is quite close to the state of transcendental wisdom. Both forgiving love and transcendental wisdom can only be achieved through a deep understanding of the origins of the universe, Buddha's will, the mission of human beings, the system of reincarnation and the impermanence and egolessness of all beings.

6

A Religious Perspective and Spiritual Refinement

I have looked at transcendental wisdom and forgiving love from several angles and now I would like to conclude with some important points that need to be kept in mind. A person who has attained a religious perspective is able to take the view that the self and others are not separate, but one, and that good and evil are inseparable. However, you should know that this understanding can only be reached after having gained a profound insight into the deeper meaning of the self and others, and of good and evil, as a result of having made tireless efforts towards spiritual development. These views are not the same as an inability to distinguish between good and evil. If you see someone who is unable to distinguish between good and evil, then you must teach them the difference. This is an extremely important lesson, because you can only transcend good and evil after having learned to distinguish between them. The distinction between good and evil must be understood in order to move to a higher level where the distinction can be transcended. To know the difference between good and evil, you have to make a thorough study of what good and evil are.

For this reason, transcendental wisdom does not refer to a simple, good-natured attitude which sees everything as good, nor does it refer to confusion about good and evil. It does not provide any excuses for laziness when it comes to spiritual refinement. The state of transcendental wisdom embodies a great enlightenment, where you endeavour to see the whole picture from a broad perspective with a mind that constantly seeks to be egoless and a heart which constantly draws close to the void.

If you misunderstand this, if everything becomes confused and you then conclude that there is no such thing as good or evil, or that good religions are indistinguishable from the misguided ones, it means you are headed in a wrong direction and could end up falling off a steep cliff while under the illusion that you are on the right path and headed in the direction of progress and evolution. Remember that transcendental wisdom can only be attained as the result of constant effort to refine your soul. Watch that you do not become conceited.

CHAPTER FIVE

The Benefits of An Egoless Perspective

1

The True Meaning of Egolessness

Time and again I have given lectures on egolessness and some of you may wonder why I am discussing such an old-fashioned idea at this time, or why I speak repeatedly on such an abstract idea. Others may not understand why it is so important, although they may be familiar with the term 'egolessness'. To answer these questions, I would like to talk about the benefits of an egoless perspective. It may seem a rather unusual topic for Buddhist writings, but it is my intention to discuss not only the concept of egolessness but also its benefits, or the benefits of having views based on it.

Buddhists are usually rather reluctant to explain the practical benefits of following Buddha's teachings. Unlike pharmacists who advertise the effects of certain medicines,

Buddhists are inclined to avoid explaining the benefits of practising Buddhism. Although there are many religions that attempt to attract people by advertising the worldly benefits that will accrue through the practice of their teachings, very few attempt to explain traditional Buddhist concepts such as egolessness from a practical point of view. While I am well aware of the current situation, I would like to discuss why you should study egolessness from a pragmatic point of view and what the results of studying it will be.

To put it simply, egolessness is a teaching that tells you that the ego, or who you think you are, does not exist. However, I expect that some of you might argue, 'You said the ego does not exist, but look, here I am. If I were to hit the person in front of me and tell him he is not feeling any pain because his ego does not really exist, he would still feel pain.' For this reason they may conclude my definition is wrong.

Some people interpret egolessness to mean that when you die everything disappears. Some may question how egolessness is possible while we live in this world. Others adopt a materialistic viewpoint, arguing that because the human body consists of atoms and molecules which will ultimately decompose and turn into carbon dioxide and water, it follows that human beings have no real substance. Yet others think that there is no such thing as the human mind; rather, they believe that only the functioning of the brain and the nervous system exist. All these arguments are misguided.

Many complex philosophies have developed around the argument about whether or not the ego really exists. However, to begin the discussion in this chapter, I would at least like you to understand that the egolessness *Shakyamuni Buddha* taught was not a simple denial of the existence of the ego.

Shakyamuni Buddha taught of the importance of spiritual refinement and in his sermons he never said things like, 'You do not exist' or 'I do not exist'. Had this been the case, there would be no need for discipline, no need to make an effort and no need to maintain an attitude of commitment to practices. To interpret egolessness in terms of the existence or non-existence of self would go against his last message before he left this earthly world, 'Everything is transient, so do not become attached to anything; do not be lazy, but constantly refine your soul.' If egolessness is interpreted as the denial of the existence of the self, it is like saying, 'When you die, everything will disappear, nothing will remain', and *Shakyamuni*'s last words to encourage his disciples in the diligent disciplining and refining of the self would have been groundless.

2

The Torch Within and the Torch of Dharma

*S*hakyamuni once said:

I am like the moon. Even though the moon may seem to disappear behind the clouds, it still continues shining brightly. When the wind blows the clouds away, the moon will appear once again, perfectly round. Just as the full moon is gradually covered by cloud, my life may now seem to be disappearing from your sight, as I am dying. However, this is temporary and it does not mean that I will completely disappear or be lost forever. In fact, like the moon I will always continue to shine as brightly as ever. For a while I will be hidden from you, but there is a purpose to this. If I were to light this world constantly, you would fail to light the torch within you and you would not be able to illuminate your own path. This is why I am disappearing from you, my disciples. Understand that this does not mean that I have gone forever or that I have ceased to exist.

This was *Shakyamuni*'s teaching as he passed away. He said, 'After I die, live your lives according to what I have taught: light the torch within you and light the torch of Dharma.' To light the torch within is to illuminate yourself through your own efforts and to rely upon yourself.

In Buddhist tradition, this idea was explained in the following way. When it rains in India, it rains violently. When rivers overflow, the surrounding area will often turn into a kind of ocean, flooding almost all the small islands. Here and there, however, pieces of land remain above water providing animals with high ground on which they can survive the flood. The flood here represents the desires and suffering of human beings.

When you are drowning amidst the swirling of human desire and the suffering of this world on Earth, take refuge on the small island that is yourself; this is what you must stand on. Always live relying on yourself. After I die there will come a flood tide carrying debris. However, like the creatures that seek refuge on the small expanses of land that remain above water, you must protect your own island. Rely upon yourself.

This reveals that what *Shakyamuni* taught his disciples in his last moments on Earth was a long way from the sort of faith which involves the complete abandonment of one's own efforts and trusting in an outside power. He did not teach his disciples to worship him to attain salvation after his death. Instead, he taught them: 'Rely upon yourself, for each of you has Buddha-nature within. As you continue to live your lives, it will guide you.'

As well as the torch within, *Shakyamuni Buddha* left behind the 'torch of Dharma'. He taught that after his death, the disciples should live according to his teachings, because although they would have understood that they must rely upon themselves, when it came to solving day-to-day problems, there would be certain situations they would not know how to deal with. Wishing to turn to their teacher for guidance, he would not be there, in the same way as the moon is hidden behind clouds. *Shakyamuni* taught his disciples that on such occasions they should base their decisions on the teachings that he had left for them. This shows clearly that *Shakyamuni*, even in the last days of his life of eighty years, still placed much importance on a way of life that was not passive, through constantly refining the self, trusting the self and observing the Dharma as a guide.

3

Teachings to Develop the Self that is One with Buddha

Buddhism teaches concepts such as the impermanence of all worldly things, the egolessness of all creation and the perfect tranquility of nirvana. Some people may misunderstand these ideas, seeing them as negative and gloomy, and conclude that Buddhism is a religion of weakness. A certain Japanese psychologist claimed that 'Christianity is an aggressive religion, whereas Buddhism is passive. If you were to psychoanalyse *Shakyamuni*, you would discover that as a person, he was weak.'

People who think like this might interpret 'all things are impermanent' to mean that everything in this world is an empty dream and will be carried away by death. Or they might think 'all things are without ego' to mean that nothing in this world is substantial, so that neither they

themselves nor anyone else really exist. They may then conclude that Buddhists are pessimistic and nihilistic. If this were
true, it would be no wonder Buddhism was regarded as a
passive religion. However, this interpretation of Buddhism is
completely wrong.

Remember that when *Shakyamuni* was departing this
world at the age of eighty, after more than forty years of total
dedication to teaching and spreading the law, he taught his
disciples, 'Always refine your soul. Live according to the
Dharma. Do not depend on me but rely on yourself, and be
devoted to the Buddha within you.' This shows that
Buddhism is actually a very proactive religion.

Buddhism preaches a boundless trust in the individual, in
the soul and in the commitment to refining the soul. This
continual effort to refine one's soul is the driving force.
Buddha urges you to drive your ship forward using your
own propellers. Are these the teachings of a weak religion?
Quite the opposite.

The point that I am trying to make here is that egolessness
has nothing to do with the view that death will sweep away
everything, it has nothing to do with any lack of energy or
strength. On the contrary, Buddhism is a teaching to develop
a truly strong, radiant self that is one with Buddha. When you
become truly one with Buddha, you will cease to be a weak
human being of this world; instead you will be empowered
by a strength previously unknown to you. You will acquire
the power of enlightenment enabling you to dissolve all your
worldly suffering, pain and attachments outright.

You may have noticed that the statue of Buddha is often

accompanied by a statue of Manjushri, the Bodhisattva who represents wisdom and holds a sword, 'the sharp sword of Manjushri'.* This sword represents the power of wisdom to cut through all worldly bonds and attachments. It cuts away all obstacles on the path to enlightenment.

You can acquire this sharp sword of Manjushri through continuous spiritual refinement. You will be given great power through the process of abandoning all sorts of worldly seductions and attachments, by overcoming various difficulties, disciplining your mind and developing your spiritual strength. This power becomes like a spiritual sword that allows you to cut away any problems that may stand in your way. It is also the sword that quells evil. Not only is the sword able to cut away desires, attachments and seductions, it can also conquer evil. This sword is a rudder too, guiding you in the right direction as you are carried downstream.

---

* Manjushri was a disciple of *Shakyamuni Buddha* who, after *Shakyamuni*'s death, went to southern India to convey the Buddha's teachings. Her activities became the source of the Mahayana Movement in Buddhism.

4

Egolessness – The Determining Factor for Heaven or Hell

My experiences of the other world reminded me how essential the teaching of egolessness is. Before I acquired my spiritual gifts, even if I had made an academic study of the teaching of egolessness, the limits of my understanding would have been that egolessness is simply a recommendation to control one's ego because over-assertiveness offends other people. However, as someone who has experienced the world beyond, I cannot stress enough the importance of the concept of egolessness.

The world after death can be classified in two major realms: heaven and hell. I have met many people who are in hell and I have listened to what they said. All of them were experiencing suffering and pain. Whether they themselves were aware of it or not is another matter, but their suffering was obvious to the ordinary person. They were suffering in a realm filled with destruction, violence, attachment, confusion, bewilderment, jealousy, envy, a realm where malicious battles rage for the sake of satisfying greed. All spirits in hell are concerned only with themselves and seeking their own happiness, but they cannot escape from suffering. Being unable to close the gap between their desire for happiness and the reality of their agony, their dissatisfaction only escalates. Then they blame others and their environment for their misery. While they so desperately seek to satisfy their desires, these spirits are actually tormenting themselves.

What is so pitiful about these spirits is that they are all self-centred. They are concerned solely with 'me'. If only they could abandon what they believe themselves to be, they could be happy, but they are unable to do so. What they think of as the 'self' is not the spiritual self. It is not the self that receives Buddha's light, nor is it part of Buddha's light, but rather it is the 'ego' self which has been strongly influenced and conditioned by this three-dimensional world. It is the 'self' formed by the environment in which one grows up, the education one receives, and the particular ways of thinking and beliefs one has been influenced by. It is the 'self' that is defined by the place of birth, family background, education, work, status, income, spouse and so on.

I have seen spirits in hell who insisted, 'I am a government minister, so I cannot accept the way I am being treated now.' 'I am the president of a large corporation. Why doesn't someone come to meet me with a car?' It was truly dreadful. Another person was shouting, 'I am the prime minister.

Why am I being treated in this way? I will not forgive you! Is there anyone there? Come here, quickly!' All were too self-centred to understand what was wrong, or where they were.

In contrast, those people who have returned to heaven are living in harmony. All of them truly care for one another. They live extending love to one another and all of them are happy. They restrain from taking love from others and are kind to each other. It is a community of happy, smiling people. In the realm of Bodhisattva, a stage higher, people are totally devoted to the happiness of others. People there lead active lives, concerned only with giving. Ordinary people tend to think that 'when I give, I lose something, when I am given to, I gain'. However, this thinking is fundamentally wrong.

In this material world, it is true that if you give something away, your possessions are reduced, and if you are given something your possessions increase by that amount. For example, if someone gives you a thousand dollars you will gain that amount, while the person who gave it to you will lose the same amount. In the three-dimensional world, the person who gives to others loses, while the person who is given to gains. However, in the spirit world, the result is the complete opposite. The more you give to others, the happier you will be. The more you devote yourself to others, the more happiness you will receive.

The reason for this is that you are expanding yourself as a child of Buddha. The closer you draw to Buddha, the more light you will radiate as the child of Buddha. The light you give out means an enhanced feeling of happiness and the expansion of your 'self'. You can feel that you are growing and that you are approaching Buddha. This is true happiness.

In short, happiness in the other world is a spiritual happiness. Spiritual happiness means drawing closer to Buddha. You can feel happiness when you feel yourself growing. Take children, for example. Happiness for them is finding that they are growing year by year. They feel happy as they become taller and heavier, as their knowledge increases and they make friends at school. In the spirit world, too, you can feel happiness when you grow. It is not the happiness of growing physically, but the happiness of approaching Buddha, the source of all light. Instead of growing heavier, you become lighter, like the fresh breezes of May. To enjoy a feeling of lightness, you have to get rid of your attachment to 'I', 'me' and 'mine'.

Love is a very important part of our spiritual refinement while we are living on Earth. There are many types of love – the love of lovers, the love of a husband and wife, the love between a parent and child, also neighbourly love. However, love has two sides. If you love others in the wrong way, your love may bind them. The love of others can be either gentle or harsh; it is the two different sides of love that create heaven and hell.

A parent's love for a child is not a love that expects any reward or recompense. However, if a parent tries to bind a child, becoming greedy or possessive, or makes the child do things for him or her, in short, if a parent tries to use a child for his or her own ends, this love may change into wrong love or what is thought of as love in hell. So long as a parent gives love to a child without expecting any return, the child will be grateful and feel like giving something back to the parent. However, if the parent takes care of the child in the hope of getting something from the child, then this will change into taking love, and this will cause the child to rebel.

In this world, too, giving or taking love will bring similar consequences to those in the other world. In this world, the giver is said to lose, while the person who receives is said to gain. However, the owner of a business working with the intention of delivering quality merchandise to customers will ultimately prosper. On the other hand, someone who is always on the lookout for the slightest chance of making a profit through cheating, by taking advantage of others or deceiving them will lose the trust of customers in the end, although at the outset the business may appear to be successful. When someone can no longer survive in business, he or she is likely to start taking advantage of others. This type of person concentrates on depriving others.

A similar thing happens in religions. While some religions work as hard as they can to bring happiness to large numbers of people, many pursue only worldly interests and seek to control others to satisfy their greed. It may seem that many of these sorts of religions thrive in today's world. However, you need to understand how important it is to see whether a religion is based on a willingness to give to others. Whether the founder and followers of a religion have the sincere desire to bring happiness to others, or whether they are only seeking to satisfy their own desires for power and control will determine the direction in which that religion leads people, to heaven or to hell.

Now you may have understood why *Shakyamuni Buddha* taught the idea of egolessness again and again. He taught that people need to be selfless and free themselves from attachment to worldly possessions. The true purpose of the teaching of egolessness is not only to save yourself but also to prevent you from creating a hell around you.

5

Advice on Egolessness

i Egolessness does not mean suppressing individuality

One point you should not forget is that egolessness does not mean you should suppress your individuality. Becoming egoless does not mean becoming characterless. Egolessness does not imply that everyone loses their identity, becoming bland like jelly; this would be contrary to the true will of Buddha.

Look at the wealth of plant and animal species. Buddha appreciates the development and prosperity of individuals that create the artistry of the world as a whole. He values highly the process by which the individual endeavours to contribute to the formation of the divine world, each in their own way based on the spirit of self-responsibility. An intelligent person uses their brain, someone who is robust uses their physical strength; every individual should contribute their light and participate in the creation of heaven by doing what they can, a woman as a woman, a man as a man, parents as parents, a child as a child, and an old person as an old person. It is very important to respect the individuality of each person.

Egolessness certainly does not mean people should be characterless. Expressing one's individuality does not imply taking from or depriving others, rather, it is a process of illuminating the world with your own unique light. Individuality is like a searchlight, a torch, or the light of a candle. There are many candles and they burn with flames of different shapes and colours, but when each of those unique lights attempts to illuminate the world, an ideal world will emerge.

ii Do not allow the egos of others to become inflated

I would now like to raise one more point to bear in mind in relation to egolessness. Within the Sangha, or the Buddha's order, fellow members have a mutual understanding based on Buddha's Truth and they can create an ideal world following the teachings of egolessness, restraining their own desires and living for the benefit of others. However, you should be aware that the teaching of egolessness could be harmful in the face of those who are still ignorant and have not yet entered the world of the Sangha. Your egoless attitude should not cause other people's egos to inflate, but occasionally this does seem to happen.

Those who understand Buddha's Truth can understand and give to one another. However, to a person who has absolutely no knowledge of Buddha's Truth and thinks in a completely different way, in other words, in a way that leads to hell, those who do not have egos sometimes appear simple-minded and easy to deceive. Someone who will take advantage of this is like a wolf among sheep.

You must fully understand that in being egoless you should not mislead those who try to take advantage of you, who deceive or steal, causing their egos to become inflated; this is like pouring oil on fire. It is a question of wisdom. If you possess wisdom, you will never try to add to the sum of suffering; rather, you will try and reduce it. If you possess wisdom, you will try never to add to the sum of human mistakes; rather you will try to reduce them. So if you wish to become wise, you must not encourage those who do wrong, who are already committing crimes or are about to, adding to their sins or bad karma. You must stop them from making a mistake.

There are two ways of stopping them. First, you should always be on your guard so that your egolessness, your attitude of giving love as if you were in the heavenly world, does not encourage other people's wrong desires. When you are dealing with people who have a strong egocentric mind-set, you should keep a certain distance from them if you do not think it is the right time to invite them to join your group. Letting a wolf loose among a flock of sheep and saying 'we are sheep' is not wise. You must be cautious and keep your distance from wolves. This attitude is not born of

selfish desire nor does it imply that you are presen
ego. It is simply important to have this wisdom. S
you think a person is gradually awakening to the truth,
then you should give adequate guidance little by little, to
satisfy that person's needs.

iii Do not humble yourself too much

Essentially, egolessness brings humility and gratitude.
However, there are some people who allow humility and
gratitude to lead to self-depreciation. You should not make
this mistake; putting yourself down or humiliating yourself is
not egolessness. Thinking that humility leads to gratitude,
some people put themselves down, but this attitude only
causes others to elevate their position relative to you. As a
result, you may mistakenly cause others to look down on you
and consequently cause them to become conceited. You must
exercise caution, distinguishing between 'remaining humble'
and 'being weak' for there is an enormous difference.

iv Give with wisdom

There is a risk of turning the idea of egolessness into a mistaken form of giving love which could lead others to
downfall. You must not lead others on with sugared words,
for instance, 'I can give you everything you want' which
may result in their over-indulgence. On the other hand, there

is also a risk that your egoless attitude may be merely self-abasing, which discourages you and turns others into egotists who understand neither self-reflection nor humility.

Despite the fact that egolessness is a concept associated with heaven, unless you use wisdom it can lead others in the wrong direction. You must not put the idea of egolessness into practice in a way that will increase other people's wrongdoing or cause them to make new mistakes. This is where you need to apply wisdom. In this case, wisdom is like 'the sharp sword of Manjushri'. It is important to put a stop to others' wrong desires, point out their errors, and avoid putting yourself in the position of leading others in a wrong direction.

You have to be strong, not in a worldly sense on your own account but as a true self, who is of service to Buddha. What is most important is that the work of Buddha advances each day. Do not apply the idea of egolessness in any way that will disturb the work of Buddha.

6

Egolessness and Spiritually Nurturing Love

First of all, it is important to control your own ego and your self-centred desires. Pride, being too competitive, looking down on others – these tendencies are all ugly so we need to control them and seek to live in harmony with one another. We have to watch ourselves and also prevent those who have not yet reached a level where they are able to control themselves from going in the wrong direction. Do not apply the idea of egolessness in a wrong way which will increase the egotism of others, but be disciplined and use wisdom in the face of wrong action. To point out what is wrong when someone makes a mistake is a form of love. To give stern guidance is also love – it is called spiritually nurturing love.

If you give love without wisdom, it may mislead others. Love must evolve to a higher level, to the level of spiritually nurturing love that guides others in the right direction. In order to be able to guide others properly, it is important to understand the difference between good and evil. You need to know what is wrong to be able to choose what is right. If you are unable to distinguish good from evil you will not be able to create what is good. You must be able to tell the difference. If you know what is wrong, you will not dirty yourself, and you will stay away from evil even if it is within easy grasp. Through this striving, goodness is realised.

Do not misunderstand egolessness, thinking it means you are easily influenced by both good and evil. Being egoless means keeping yourself untainted, as if you were a plain white cloth. It is easy for a white cloth to become stained, but to be egoless does not mean to be susceptible to staining. Whenever the cloth becomes dirty, you should wash it. The constant effort to keep a cloth white represents your constant efforts to do your best to increase the radiance within you. I would like you to think about how you can put egolessness into practice to improve yourself and society as a whole.

CHAPTER SIX

Practising the Middle Way

1

Avoiding Extremes

I would now like to explain how to practise 'the Middle Way', focusing on its use in everyday life, rather than trying to interpret this concept simply as a theory. A definition of the Middle Way perhaps suggests to you a path which appears in the centre after excluding two extremes; in fact, it is easy enough to understand the term 'the Middle Way' by focusing on the concept of avoiding extremes.[5] Sometimes the Middle Way is symbolically expressed by a gesture — hands with palms pressed together in prayer. But if you actually try to put the Middle Way into practice in daily life you may wonder what these extremes actually are, so I will start by explaining what is meant by the extremes that should be

---

5   Refer to *The Laws of the Sun*, chapters four and six, ibid.

avoided. The purpose of the concept of the Middle Way is, after all, to eliminate suffering and enjoy a peaceful state of mind. So the extremes to be avoided are conditions that cause us suffering, and the causes of this suffering are in actual fact closely related to the condition of our bodies and our state of mind.

2

Blaming the Outside World and Blaming the Inner Self

First, let us take a look at some problems of the mind. In what situations do you feel pain? There are, for instance, two extreme cases – when you blame the outside world and when you blame yourself. What does it mean to blame the outside world? It means blaming others or your surroundings for your distress and unhappiness. In these cases, your mind is filled with hatred, anger, jealousy, envy and suspicion. From the viewpoint of the spirit world, it appears as if arrows of criticism are constantly being released toward others out of your mind, your eyes and your mouth. This is one extreme.

When you are in this state of mind, you will perceive everyone else as being in the wrong and you will be unable to stop criticising others and speaking ill of them. You will be obsessed by the thought, 'he is to blame' or 'she is to blame', and your environment or social conditions may also be a target of your blame. Of course, your criticisms are sometimes valid; you may well be confronted by serious problems because of other people. In such cases, you will need to use wisdom to solve these difficulties.

Frequently we are faced with difficulties that cause us to suffer, for instance in natural disasters and economic recessions. You might blame an earthquake, a tsunami, a forest fire, a flood, a drought or a famine for your suffering. For some reason, the oil supply may be cut off, your business may suffer a downturn, or a whole industry that you are a part of may fall apart, and so on. There are, in fact, many situations that you as an individual can do nothing about – some are actually beyond human control – so it is not always a mistake to recognise these as the causes of your suffering.

At times it is true that you suffer as a result of changes in external conditions. But looking at these outside factors, you should ask yourself whether you can change them through your own efforts. If you think you can, there is still room for you to make an effort. For example, imagine that you are a mother with a young child. If the baby does something wrong, you can chide the baby and correct its mistake. Instead of simply complaining and worrying about your child's behaviour, you can choose to do something proactive to rectify it, such as pointing out the mistake and warning the child not to do the same thing again.

However, in cases that involve the whole of society, things are not so simple. In these situations you first need to realise that just worrying or complaining about other people or your environment is not productive. Next, you should ask yourself if there is anything you can do about the situation. Is there a way to get ashore, to cross a torrent of pain using your own paddle? Approaching a situation in this way is more productive than listing your causes for complaint.

On the other hand, your mind may go in the direction of blaming, punishing or tormenting yourself. This is the second of the two extremes, and this attitude is also wrong because it may eventually cause you to doubt that you are the child of Buddha. As I have said over and over again, it is true that no matter how miserable the conditions, no matter how much pain and sorrow you are experiencing, Buddha is constantly pouring out His great love to each of you. Even if you are now suffering in a deep chasm of agony, warm eyes are still watching over you. Sometimes people are judged good or bad as a result of their thoughts and deeds. You may even find yourself labelled 'bad', but still Buddha continues pouring out the light of the sun and showering the rain of compassion on every person, regardless of whether they are good or have made mistakes.

When you feel truly grateful for the great compassion of Buddha and come to realise the true dignity of your own being, this is a good time to make a decision to transform and improve yourself, correcting your shortcomings through self-reflection. This is a very positive attitude and it is commendable. But if you are too hard on yourself and start becoming self-deprecating, saying or thinking 'I am good for nothing', you will become discouraged and negative. You will then try to win the sympathy of others, be obsessed by an inferiority complex, be unable to trust others, avoid meeting people, and in the end live like a hermit, still dissatisfied and grumbling. This is certainly a state to be avoided.

Whereas the first extreme, blaming outside factors, is aggressive, the latter seems somewhat passive. Although self-reflection is important, we must not dwell on negatives but instead focus on the dignity of being. Some of those who have been raised in Christian environments have difficulty getting away from the idea that human beings are born sinful and they consider their origins to be sinful. There are also particular groups of people who even see themselves to be the children of Satan and believe satanic blood is flowing through their veins. This is sad because it lessens their chances of being truly happy.

As we have seen, there are two extremes: an attitude of aggressive attack on the outside world and a tendency to humiliate oneself, even sometimes to the extent of driving oneself to spiritual suicide. Neither way leads to happiness. The Middle Way is a state of mind which avoids these extremes. I would like you to remember this as a way of controlling your mind in everyday life. In short, you must not attribute too much happiness or unhappiness to outside factors and, at the same time, you must not take too much responsibility for the unhappiness of yourself or others to the extent that you destroy yourself or deny your Buddha-nature.

3

Buddha-Nature Appears Through the Middle Way

Essentially, human beings have a divine nature, or Buddha-nature, within. It is the diamond at the core of our soul, and it can also be understood as the nature that enables us to attain enlightenment. We are such precious beings. However, as we live on Earth in a physical body, controlled by the six sense organs – the eyes, the ears, the nose, the tongue, the tactile body and the mind – and as we are influenced by other people's opinions, our social circumstances, educational background or business environment, our views gradually become distorted which eventually leads to suffering. The root of our suffering lies in mistaken thoughts and actions which originate from what we have absorbed from this world.

Although you should not forget that you are essentially a being of great value, you also need to remember that the cause of suffering is to be found in your own thoughts and actions. You are basically a good, blessed being, but when your thinking or your actions are mistaken you create suffering. Once you avoid clinging to any extreme, the state of mind known as the Middle Way appears. It is a harmonious state in which you do not harm yourself or others. It is also the state of mind which can create an ideal society. Happiness is not born through denying your own values or criticising others. The intention of making an effort to live in harmony with others will lead to an ideal society and this is also the Middle Way.

What kind of attitudes characterise the Middle Way? We can start with consideration for others, modesty, kindness, thoughtfulness, the willingness to make an effort, gratitude and faith. The Middle Way is also characterised by a loving and harmonious heart, a heart that feels gratitude to others, leading you to co-operate with them, while remaining humble. However, as you live in this world on Earth, your mind gradually becomes covered over with 'rust', so every day you need to remove this 'rust'. With daily practice, you can enter a path where you will harm neither yourself nor others.

Self-reflection is the practice of constantly removing the rust from your mind. In practising self-reflection what is required of you is humility. You can correct your mistakes only if you are humble. If there is no humility, the six worldly delusions – greed, anger, foolishness, pride, doubt and false views – will play havoc with your mind. You can free yourself from these delusions if you can discover your true self and know that you are the child of Buddha. If you cannot honestly see yourself as you really are, all sorts of desires and suffering will arise. You will be carried away by your own greed or by other people's opinions and evaluations, gradually losing sight of your true self, and as a result you will suffer.

4

Harmonising Body and Spirit

So far, I have explained the Middle Way from a spiritual perspective. Now, let me proceed to another important point in the practice of the Middle Way, which is 'harmonising body and spirit'. This is actually the most important point of all.

There is an extreme philosophy that asserts 'human beings are only flesh, and they live in a world that consists only of matter'. This view is materialistic, valuing only the material world. On the other hand, there are people who are excessively absorbed in the Buddhist philosophy of the 'void' or 'emptiness', and who deny the things of this world completely. Although they have a religious disposition, they are so eager to abandon this world that they fall into the trap of nihilism. However, if everyone were to become like this, this world could never become like heaven. Instead, hell would unfold right here. If people thought of nothing except how to escape from this world, it would never be an ideal world.

Although the spirit world really does exist, it is not right to deny the meaning of this earthly world completely, or to try and ignore it. Materialistic views and spiritual views are two extremes, but neither can be avoided completely as long as we live in this world. For this reason it is all the more important to seek a balanced view of both, and a harmony of body and spirit.

In Buddhism, the phrase 'mind and matter are one' expresses this balance. This means that the body and the spirit cannot be completely separated. Let us look into this further. I once read a book written by one of the Japanese Zen masters, the self-appointed successor of the Buddhist scholar Daisetsu Suzuki (1870–1966 CE). This Zen master explained that the body and mind are one, so when the body perishes, the mind perishes too. In short, he says that when a body is cremated, the mind also vanishes into thin air. But this view is the equivalent of the idea that when a person dies, everything comes to an end. Actually, it is one of the 'false views' *Shakyamuni Buddha* disapproved of. It seems the Zen master did not understand this, the reasons being that he himself was unable to recognise spiritual beings and that he did not have faith in Buddha. He devoted himself solely to a physical training with a materialistic perspective and, as a result, ended up with a miserably low level of enlightenment. I would like you to remember that extreme views on the relationship between the body and the mind actually do exist.

5

Self-Reflection – Acquiring a Spiritual Perspective

As you continue in your efforts to improve yourself and try to remove the 'rust' from your mind, you will begin to feel the light of Buddha and receive guidance from your guardian and guiding spirits. Having reached this level, you will truly know that there is an infinite world beyond this third dimension. Then you will realise that your brother and sister souls have been constantly watching over you since you were born into this world, even though you may have thought you were undergoing your spiritual discipline alone.

You may have had good thoughts and bad thoughts, but whenever you did something wrong your spiritual brothers and sisters were watching over you from a distant world with tears in their eyes. You will realise, 'A spiritual being has been watching over me all this time. This spirit is not completely separate from me but is my true self which is within me, my authentic self, a purity of heart that lies in my subconscious. My guardian spirit represents this and has been watching over me.' Actually, the pure heart within you has constantly been watching over you as you undergo your spiritual discipline in this three-dimensional world.

Usually the subconscious lies hidden beneath the surface consciousness. While you are awake the surface consciousness is active, from the time you wake in the morning until you go to bed at night. It is not completely independent of the workings of the brain, the nervous system and other physical organs as they interact with each other. Consequently, it is very susceptible to third-dimensional, materialistic vibrations and is easily influenced by other people. Although the surface consciousness is part of the mind, it is easily affected by the vibrations of this world on Earth.

Imagine a crystal-clear lake. When autumn comes and leaves fall, the surface of the lake becomes covered with leaves and other debris and looks messy. Although the water is clear, the surface does not look clean. This resembles the surface consciousness of a person living in this world of matter and undergoing spiritual discipline. In autumn I once stayed at an inn deep in the mountains; nearby there was a small stream. In the morning, I awoke to a rustling sound. Wondering what the noise was, I looked down from my window and saw a man from the inn raking up the fallen leaves that had collected on top of the stream. Unless the leaves were swept away, you could not see the clear stream.

This story is one way of explaining the meaning of the self-reflection that I constantly recommend. Although the surface consciousness is basically connected to the subconscious, it becomes covered over by worldly thoughts. Unless you sweep them away, you cannot see the truth. Your guardian spirit is always watching over you, wanting you to hear his or her true voice, but if your surface consciousness is still dirty or cloudy, your guardian spirit will have difficulty contacting you.

As the clouds over the surface consciousness are cleared away one at a time through self-reflection, communication with your subconscious becomes easier. What happens then? You will be connected to the Real World, even though you still live in a physical body. Your thoughts will coincide with the thoughts of your guardian spirit. This means you will be able to see things from the viewpoint of the Real World. As you live from a spiritual perspective, your own problems and worries will gradually disappear.

In this age, most people worry constantly about making decisions – what to do, which alternative to choose, when to do something, whether to do it now, tomorrow, in a year and so on. However, when you are attuned to your guardian spirit, you can get the answers from the perspective of your guardian spirit, and you may find that your desires were misleading you. If you want to make a decision about changing jobs, getting married or about a business matter, your guardian spirit can give you the inspiration to make a choice that is better for your life. However, if your worldly desires or your attachment to the things of this world are too strong, you will make wrong decisions and choose a wrong direction.

6

Knowing How to Be Content

I have said that self-reflection is important. So what is needed to clear surface consciousness and to stay in contact with your subconscious? One attitude that is essential is knowing how to be content.

While we live in this world on Earth it is not so easy to control our desires and stop them from increasing. We want to get more and more things. We may become arrogant. When we find ourselves in this sort of state, it is a good idea to reflect on ourselves, focusing on how we can be content. 'I have been allowed to live today. I did not die of starvation. Although many things happened, I managed to live one day, the Earth did not disintegrate, the sun did not stop shining, and I did not lack food. I may have had various problems and worries, but I lived through today. There have been many days before this, and there will almost certainly be a tomorrow . . .'

Reflect in this way and feel thankful that you are blessed with each day. Instead of aiming too high, love your life as it is now. You may not be totally satisfied with your present situation if you compare it to someone else's, but there is no telling whether the person you feel envious of is truly satisfied. Each person has his or her own problems to face and some of the people you hold in low regard may actually be leading wonderful lives.

Each person leads their own life. Knowing how to be content means loving your life and embracing it. The desire for material things knows no end and the same is true of the desire for money, the desire for status, the desire for fame and the desire for sex. If a married couple who love each other raise a family and live in harmony for some decades, they are actually living the Middle Way, knowing how to be content. On the other hand, there is no end to the number of people you see who never learn how to be content, who indulge in extramarital affairs and destroy their family. They are well aware of what will happen if they behave in this way, but they are unable to control their desires and as a result their family is destroyed.

It takes nearly thirty years for a couple to raise children, so it is extremely important to maintain the stability of the family for thirty years. If this stability is destroyed, the future of the children will be affected and the parents' lives may also stray in the wrong direction. I would like to stress that to prevent a family from breaking up, knowing how to be content is essential.

In *Shakyamuni Buddha*'s time in India, disciples were not allowed to have a family of their own. Today, however, even clergy and those who practise religion have families of their own, so conditions for practising the Middle Way are much more favourable today than in the past. Clergy and lay people alike are allowed to have families and lead ordinary lives; each day can be valuable and precious. To keep a marriage from breaking up, a husband and a wife need to be thankful and appreciate one another's good points day in and day out, finding happiness in bringing up children together. Looking for another man or woman who has the qualities your spouse does not possess will never lead to true happiness.

Knowing how to be content is, in truth, the key to achieving the greatest happiness in life. I would like you to remember that the way to ensure domestic happiness in these times is to know how to be content and live according to the Middle Way. On the foundations of a secure family life, business life flourishes. In business, you may not always be as successful as others. You may feel inferior to someone you admire or hold as your model. However, you should ask yourself what the purpose of your spiritual refinement in this lifetime is, what your assignment is. Then be determined to do the very best you can to solve the problems assigned to you in this lifetime.

I also recommend this way of thinking: 'In the next life I will undergo a different kind of spiritual development, but in this life I was born into this environment and chose this job. It may be rather difficult to change my job completely, so I will achieve as much as I can with what I have in this lifetime.' It is no use for a farmer to envy a fisherman, or for a fisherman to be envious of a farmer. When you are determined to achieve the best possible results from your spiritual development in this lifetime in your present occupation, the way to true development and prosperity will open up.

If you live the Middle Way and know how to be content you can avoid coming under negative spiritual influences. Always be on your guard and you will be able to escape possession by the stray spirits that roam the streets and gather round misleading religions. Even if you are told that the cause of your sufferings is your ancestors who are still not able to return to heaven, if you live in harmony on this Earth, they will not have the chance to disturb you.* Looking at the harmonious life that you, their descendant, leads, they will reflect on themselves with tears of repentance. In this way, their situation will also improve.

First, protect your own mind from evil while you are living the Middle Way and know how to be content. Next, fill your home with the light of harmony to prevent evil or stray spirits from invading your family. It is greed that leaves you unguarded. Quarrels and strong, uncontrollable desires

---

* Ancestor worship is popular in Japan and other Buddhist countries, and people perform ritual services for their ancestors. In Buddhism, there is an idea of saving people who have passed away before knowing the Truth, and a ritual service for ancestors is believed to be one way of saving them. However, some misguided religions take this opportunity to threaten people, putting all the blame for misfortune on their ancestors. This gives rise to many problems.

invite their attack, so be determined always to control your desires and walk the Middle Way together with your family. Be on your guard against evil, never let it enter your home. This is the path that promises you happiness for all eternity; it is the path of spiritual development that you should walk each day with steady steps.

CHAPTER SEVEN

Enlightenment and Spiritual Powers

1

Spiritual Experiences as a Precondition for Enlightenment

The main topic of this chapter is the relationship between enlightenment and spiritual powers. To begin with, I feel it is necessary to look back at my own experiences. In my case there is no denying that even before I was born into this world this was my mission, and that my spiritual leanings were an important factor. However, I have to say that my spiritual gifts and experiences played a vital role in my attaining enlightenment.

Those who can accept religious truths without doubts may think it is enough simply to accept what is written or what they hear. But in my own experience, my level of spiritual awakening and awareness changed completely after I had actually experienced the existence of spiritual beings. To know that the spirit world really did exist came

as a great surprise, even though before I experienced it I
was able to understand this fact intellectually as knowledge.

2

The Influence of Spiritual Experiences on Enlightenment

i Knowing of the existence of the spirit world and eternal life

Knowing of the spirit world influences enlightenment in stages. First of all, spiritual experiences open your eyes to the other world which lies beyond this three-dimensional world of phenomena. This is already a huge leap. All human beings while in a physical body will age and eventually die, but if they can truly perceive that the soul or 'spiritual self' lives on after death, this true knowledge will inevitably change the way they live now and in the future.

This is exactly what happened to me. I had understood the other world and reincarnation intellectually, yet it was a great surprise to learn that the spirit world actually existed and that people continue to live on as spiritual beings with the same ways of thinking and the same characteristics as if they were still alive, even though they have already left the physical body. It was also a great joy to know that no effort we make in this world is ever wasted.

If we simply died without trace at the age of seventy or eighty, what meaning would making an effort throughout our whole lives have? Why do people seek goodness? Why do people seek happiness? It seems as if there are no answers to these questions. However, if you know that there is life after death, you will truly understand what the religions, philosophies and moralities of many different countries around the world have continued to teach for thousands of years. You will understand that this life is only a period of transition until the next life. Like a caterpillar that goes into a cocoon and eventually turns into a butterfly, the soul is born into this world and returns to the other world as a butterfly. You will understand that reincarnation is like a transformation. From a spiritual viewpoint, this three-dimensional world appears to be full of restrictions, but it is like a period when we remain in a cocoon, sinking into contemplation. So knowing about the existence of the spirit world is certainly a great step toward enlightenment.

ii Understanding good and evil in the Real World

However, you cannot claim that simply by knowing of the existence of the other world you have attained enlightenment. As you have more spiritual experiences, an undeniable truth will unfold before you. You will come to know that both heaven and hell truly exist in the world after death, in the same way as both good and bad spirits exist, or spirits from heaven and spirits from hell. This may come as a great surprise or rather a shock to you.

If you contact spiritual beings, you will understand that heaven and hell, good spirits and stray spirits are divided according to a completely different values system from the one that operates in this world. You will be surprised how few people in this world know the truth. If people pursue only earthly values, it is highly possible they will fall to hell to become stray spirits; if people learned this truth, many of them would be very alarmed.

I was most surprised to see that some people who had social status, wealth, position and intelligence while they were living on Earth had gone to hell and become stray spirits. When I saw them creeping away to escape the agonies of hell, to possess people still living on Earth and driving them to madness, I could not believe that those stray spirits had once been human and had seemed refined.

On the other hand, I saw people who, although they had not been well off or achieved a great deal in this world on Earth, were enjoying happiness and total freedom in the other world. They were people who had continued to make a diligent effort, refining their hearts and minds to give out a beautiful light. I was impressed to see that such great happiness really exists.

So, the second stage of enlightenment is to know what good and evil are through contact with the spirit world.

Without this spiritual experience, or knowing the solemn reality that heaven and hell actually do exist, it is very difficult to know what good and evil really are. Through this knowledge of good and evil, you will be able to distinguish clearly good spirits from bad and heaven from hell. Then you will be able to see whether your state of mind and heart are closer to heaven or to hell and anticipate the direction in which you are likely to head after death. If you can understand this you have reached an important stage on the path to enlightenment.

To summarise, the first stage of enlightenment is knowing that life is eternal and that the other world actually exists. The next stage is understanding the distinction between good and evil which exists in the spirit world, and knowing that you will be evaluated according to your thoughts and actions during your life on Earth.

iii The relationship between the diversity of the spirit world and life on Earth

We have just discussed the second stage of enlightenment. Naturally you will be wondering whether there is a third stage – of course, there is. The third step is to learn not only of the existence of heaven and hell, but also of the diversity of human states of mind.

Hell is not a simple place; there are as many different varieties of hell as there are tendencies of the human mind. If I were to describe the characteristics of each hell, you would be able to understand easily. If you could see those who used to be aggressive, constantly harassing others, cursing and slandering, who have fallen to the Hell of Rogues, where they continue to torment each other constantly, you would understand the connection. If you could see those who were always obsessed by lust, who thought of nothing but sex and lived in a state of continual entanglement, now wriggling in the Hell of Lust or the Hell of the Bloody Pond, you would understand how being obsessed by lust is a living hell.

Those who have abandoned human dignity or who never had any respect for spirituality, who lived following materialistic desires and instincts die and go to the Hell of Beasts where they live just like animals. When you see their behaviour, it is hard to hold back the tears. However, their appearance is an exact reflection of their desires while they were living in this world. When their souls break free from the constraints of the physical body, they express themselves as animals; these animals correspond exactly to their unconscious desires. This knowledge will perhaps terrify ordinary people.

These days, those who advocate atheism and materialism may pass for smart worldly intellectuals; in fact many of these people are active in the media. However, whether or not they are aware of it, there is a clear distinction between those intellectuals who believe in the spiritual world and have lived in accordance with their faith and those who have circulated irresponsible views based on materialism, for example that there is no such thing as divinity and that humans are merely machines. Such people will fall to

Unfathomable Hell and spend day after day crying out in agony together with the souls of those who led large numbers of people astray by imbuing them with wrong thoughts. This image reminds us of the fact that living in this world we are given a great opportunity and later we will be accountable for the good and evil we do. Everything comes back to the way in which we live in this world. Actually everyone possesses a key that opens the door to all possibilities.

In heaven, too, different levels exists: the Astral Realm (the fourth dimension), the Realm of the Good-hearted (the fifth dimension) and the Light Realm (the sixth dimension) where extremely intellectual high spirits live. Higher still is the realm of the Bodhisattvas who are filled with love and compassion (the seventh dimension) and the realm of Tathagatas, the great leaders (the eighth dimension). If you would like to know Buddha, you will be able to sense His existence as you continue to ascend to higher levels in the spirit world. Heaven is so vast.

Imagine what great happiness a soul can enjoy as long as it is continuing to strive for eternal spiritual refinement in the heavenly world. At the schools in this world you have to graduate some day, but there is no graduation from schools in the other world. Once you finish a course, the next one awaits you. The process of advancement is eternal and gives rise to feelings of great joy. This joy is always accompanied by light and beauty. The world of true enlightenment is filled with happiness and joy, while hell on the other hand is filled with sorrow, despair and agony. You would be horrified to know just how big the gap is between the state of heaven and the state of hell.★

However, if you have read my books and listened to my lectures, you should be able to reach the first stage of enlightenment, the knowledge that the spirit world exists and that everyone has eternal life. It is also possible to attain the second stage of enlightenment, which is understanding spiritual values and the contrast between heaven and hell or good and evil in the light of your own experience. The third stage of enlightenment is knowing that the diversity of the spirit world with its many different levels corresponds precisely to the diverse thoughts and actions of people living in this world. If you can understand this, you have already attained quite a high level of enlightenment, considering you are still living in this world on Earth.

iv Acquiring wisdom in the three-dimensional world

So, what is the fourth stage of enlightenment? As long as you live in this world on Earth you cannot move beyond the limitation of living in a physical body. After death, you may possibly be able to live as a high spirit, free from restriction, but in this

---

★ The spirits in hell cannot be born on Earth until they have repented for their mistakes and rise to at least the Posthumous Realm in the fourth dimension of heaven. People create their own life plan before being born, but some are overwhelmed by the negative influences of the materialistic third dimension and abandon themselves to desire, resulting in their going to hell after death. However, they have chances to restart their lives any time through self-reflection and repentance.

world, you are bound by the conditions of the third dimension. As long as you live here, you cannot escape problems and worries. Day by day, week by week, month by month and year by year you are constantly confronted by problems. Unless you solve them you cannot restore a tranquillity of heart and mind or be peaceful.

Even if you have acquired some spiritual awareness or innate spiritual powers, high spirits will not come to communicate with you when you are lost in problems. As worries inevitably attract stray spirits, it is important that you solve your problems. To do this, you need to acquire wisdom, which is one of the most important objectives of living in the three-dimensional world.

As long as we are living in this three-dimensional world, we cannot live in exactly the same way as the inhabitants of the spirit world. Heaven is a world where beings live in harmony; they have none of the troubles or worries that lead to hell. On Earth, however, we face many obstacles to leading a heavenly life and directly, or indirectly through other people, we come into contact with negative spiritual influences of the hell realm where stray spirits belong. This contact brings with it worries.

Problems and anxieties need to be solved with a wisdom that can be acquired by learning Buddha's Truth. By putting this into practice, you can have the experience of solving problems and, in this way, your wisdom will develop and grow stronger. The wisdom you attain will cut through many different sorts of worries, like the sharp sword of Manjushri, the Bodhisattva who embodies wisdom. With the power of wisdom, you will be able to cut your way decisively through. In your heart and mind, you may find all sorts of attachments, one after another. However, by getting rid of these, you will always be tranquil and so reach a state of liberation.

3

The Relationship between Enlightenment and Spiritual Power

I consider enlightenment and spiritual power to be very closely related; in fact, they cannot be separated. In reality, however, there are many psychics who are not enlightened and who are manipulated and controlled by negative spiritual influences. I would call them spiritually disturbed rather than spiritually gifted persons as they are constantly possessed by stray spirits and behave as these spirits dictate. You can easily tell whether psychics have come under negative spiritual influences by examining their behaviour. In most cases, those who lead bizarre lives are controlled by stray spirits. Those who are always eccentric or outlandish in order to attract other's attention are also attuned to spirits in hell.

Psychics may start their own religion and it is easy to find out which ones have come under negative spiritual influences.

Simply look at the kinds of desires the leader has. If you can confirm that the person is concerned only with taking love from others, it means he or she has come under negative spiritual influences. If someone is always thinking about taking from others, this thought is instantly in tune with the hell realms.

In fact, to understand the spirit world, spiritual power is vital. However, it is true that such power is extremely unstable because in this three-dimensional world we can easily be affected by negative spiritual influences. So even if you acquire spiritual power, you need to remind yourself daily to lead a disciplined life, to harmonise your heart and mind, and to make a constant effort not to become proud or arrogant, otherwise you will instantly attune to the hell realms. For this reason, it is important to lead a disciplined life each day.

Unfortunately, there is no denying that more than ninety per cent of those who claim to be 'psychic' have come under negative spiritual influences. I would like you to know that spiritual power alone does not lead to the attainment of enlightenment, although this power or the knowledge acquired through it is necessary before a person can attain enlightenment.

4

The Theory of
Building a Bridge –
Enlightenment through Faith

You may also wonder whether ordinary people who do not have spiritual power can ever attain enlightenment. It is true that without direct experience it is difficult to understand the existence of the Real World. However, there is the theory of building a bridge. Even if you do not have direct experience, you can still build a bridge to the world of enlightenment by putting your faith in someone who has understood the essence of the spirit world and attained enlightenment through their spiritual gifts. It is not your own direct experience, but you can experience enlightenment through faith and this ensures your safety. Not only does it offer your soul safety and peace of mind in the three-dimensional world, it also produces the same sort of effect as if you had actually attained enlightenment.

What is the result of attaining enlightenment through faith? The basic prerequisite for seeking enlightenment is that you live in the right way that will not lead you to hell after death. Then it is important while living in this world to overcome problems and anxieties and to lead a peaceful life. The path to enlightenment means enjoying peace in this world as well as the other and aiming for the constant advancement of the soul. This being the case, the enlightenment through faith will bring results that are similar to direct experience.

5

The Zen Sect – A Long Way from Enlightenment

As far as enlightenment is concerned, many people may think that of all the sects of Buddhism, Zen is the one most closely associated with enlightenment. However, when I look at nearly two thousand years of history and examine the level of enlightenment of Zen Buddhism, I must say that very few of even the most famous Zen priests actually attained enlightenment. In the terms of Buddha's Truth as taught at our Institute, almost none of the Zen priests truly attained enlightenment. For example, the Japanese Zen priest Sojun Ikkyu (1394–1481 CE) is well known in Japan through anecdotes that reveal his sense of humour even as a child. Although he is still respected today as a quick-minded Zen priest, a close examination of his life has indicated clearly to me that he was provoked by stray spirits. He was a waggish Zen priest who was always eccentric and was influenced by rogue spirits.

There is a tendency in Zen Buddhism to think that being enlightened means behaving in a bizarre way like Ikkyu, who may appear to have been witty and eccentric. However, it is a serious mistake; this kind of life is not the goal of religious discipline. Unfortunately, the Zen sect does not have the insight to understand this crucial error.

I would like to point out another mistake made by the Zen sect in its promotion of meditation. In actual fact, Zen meditation has been reduced to mere ascetic practice. Practitioners pursue only sitting cross-legged and neglect true spirituality. In other words, their meditation is atheistic and materialistic. Those belonging to the Zen sect know little about spirituality; they believe solely that by continuing to meditate cross-legged every day, a person's will-power and meditative powers will be developed and that enlightenment is a sort of will-power to be obtained through continual ascetic practice. However, if you have studied Buddha's Truth as taught at our Institute, you will understand that the mere pursuit of will-power and physical strength does not lead to a higher level of enlightenment.

Among Zen seekers there are some who attempt to attain enlightenment through intellectual investigation alone. However, intellectual discipline by itself cannot bring enlightenment either. The main reason that the direction of the Zen sect has diverged so far from enlightenment is that none of the leaders had profound spiritual experiences. Their seeking was just sitting in meditation and working on koans, the short sentences that aim to bring students to a greater awareness of reality through contemplation.

In contrast, T'ien-t'ai Chih-i (538–597 CE), a Chinese Buddhist philosopher who had spiritual experiences, attained quite a high level of enlightenment and also had a high level of intellectual knowledge. In fact, he understood the secrets of the inner world and that thoughts can attune to every corner of the spirit world.

6

What Is True Enlightenment?

*E*nlightenment is such a difficult subject. Even if you have a channel to the spirit world, you cannot necessarily attain enlightenment. On the other hand, if you completely neglect the spirit world and merely pursue the formal practice of meditation, you are also a long way from enlightenment. If you think that you can attain enlightenment simply by contemplating the nonsense riddles posed by Zen koans, despite the fact that they were created with the aim of moving beyond the values of this world, you are also a long way from the world of truth.

Common sense applies in the world of truth and enlightenment. There are orderly systems of thought and theories. Love, compassion, courage, harmony and wisdom – wondrous ideals which can be applied in this world on Earth also apply in the other world. Today's religions, including Buddhism, are extremely confused because they can no longer understand the world of enlightenment. However, true enlightenment needs to be based not only on a knowledge of the spirit world, but must also show people living on Earth how to improve themselves steadily and constantly to ensure a peaceful life after death.

In this chapter, I have discussed the subject of enlightenment and spiritual powers. Some of you may actually wish to attain enlightenment through acquiring spiritual powers. However, your life is not limited to just this one lifetime. Each of you has experienced incarnation many times and through these experiences a particular karma, or soul tendencies, have formed. A person's tendencies might manifest as the mission to show others what enlightenment is through spiritual experiences, but this may not be your path. If it is not, instead of merely pursuing spiritual powers, determine to build a bridge with faith and walk a steady path. Now that there are true teachings about enlightenment, you can choose this great path.

CHAPTER EIGHT

What Is Karma?

1

Good and Bad Karma

The theme of this chapter is karma, a concept you may feel is rather old fashioned but it embraces a truth that is neither old nor new; karma is a Truth that is eternal. It relates to you right now.

According to Buddhism, karma is more or less synonymous with 'action', since karma is generated by actions. In order for action to occur, the function of will is always involved. When you think of doing something, that thought usually manifests as physical movement. At that moment, your thought and your action are permanently etched on the record of your life. What is created by the will and action is called karma.

Naturally, there is both 'good' karma and 'bad' karma since there are good actions as well as bad. However, karma is most often thought of as negative because it is closely related to the concept of reincarnation. Before you incarnate into this world, you prepare a rough plan of the life you are going to live on Earth. The more advanced the soul, the more complex and detailed the design of a life. Souls at lower spiritual levels tend to draw less sophisticated life plans. In any case, once you are born, you must inevitably experience all sorts of difficulties in this three-dimensional world. Faced with such difficulties, you may think they are the outcome of the karma of a past life. If you attribute your difficulties and their disastrous consequences – pain, sadness and anxiety – to the idea of past-life karma, then karma is naturally seen as negative.

However, there is a pitfall in this way of thinking. Consider looking back at your whole life. In fact, you cannot possibly claim that your life was constantly miserable, as if it rained the whole time. If you recall your life as an endless series of unhappy experiences one after another, this is just your way of remembering your life. Instead, look back over it carefully from an objective point of view, as if you were watching a movie. There must have been some good moments as well as the bad. Unfortunate events are frequently preceded by happy times.

Happiness and unhappiness arise in your life as the cumulative result of the various experiences you have had. Looking back on the last day of your life, it will be up to you to decide whether your life has been happy or not. If you think your life was unhappy, you will be recalling only the miserable experiences. On the other hand, if you think you lived a happy life, you will be recalling a lot of the good times, though you may have experienced bad times as well. So it is a question of which aspects of your life you focus on.

If you etch a tragic event very sharply on your soul, this memory may linger for decades. For example, you may be the victim of some natural disaster. If you were nearly buried or killed by a landslide but had a narrow escape, you might not manage to free yourself from this nightmare even twenty or thirty years later. That traumatic memory might have a powerful influence on your life. It all depends which images you etch on your soul.

2

Karma as a Result of Ignorance

You may question whether karma lasts through the past, present and future. The answer is yes, within certain limitations. While you cannot carry your physical body with you, when you reincarnate you can take your mind and heart, which constitute the core functions of your soul. What was etched on your mind and heart when you lived in this three-dimensional world in the past will have a great influence on your life now. If you have the kind of mentality that attracts unhappiness, you will often experience misfortune. In contrast, if you feel happy and are sensitive to happiness, you are likely to encounter many happy events.

These sorts of inclinations can be described as a kind of taste, just as you have a wide range of tastes in relation to food. You may prefer plain food to rich food; you may prefer

Japanese food to Western. You may not know why you like or dislike a certain food, but you do in fact have your own set of preferences. Similarly, your soul also has particular tastes. As a result of past incarnations you have developed certain tastes, and according to your tendencies and preferences you make choices. Strangely enough, many people choose paths that lead to unhappiness.

You may find it too simplistic to attribute the reason for such choices to the inclinations or preferences of your soul. But the reason you make poor choices can actually be attributed to 'spiritual darkness', which is described in Buddhism as the beginning of the twelve links of cause and effect that explain the suffering of human beings. This spiritual darkness means being ignorant or lacking the light of wisdom. With the light of wisdom, you are able to walk without danger, whereas if you are groping around in the dark you may trip and fall, which often happens.

People live their lives in their own way, but if someone wiser than you were placed in your position, he or she would not make the same mistakes. For example, if parents keep an eye on children, they can usually prevent them getting hurt, but left by themselves children at times fall. This happens because they do not understand the dangers. Even among adults, there are huge differences in levels of knowledge, experience and insight. You may make mistakes which could have been avoided had there been someone to give you good advice. You might find a particular situation difficult to deal with, while another person would handle it without any problem.

Looking at these examples, we see that spiritual darkness is not to be viewed as an absolute, but as relative. Depending on a person's particular situation – which involves many factors, such as ability, personal relationships, financial situation and the environment and family relationships – that person may find it extremely difficult to handle certain problems. In such cases, the person often cannot avoid making a mistake.

3

Wisdom Overcomes
Ignorance

What should we do to overcome ignorance and replace it with wisdom? As you are you will naturally continue making choices according to the particular tendencies of your soul, so it is essential to change those inclinations. In order to do this, you need to respect the views of people who have more insight than you. As I mentioned earlier, a child can avoid getting hurt if accompanied by a grown-up. From the spiritual perspective, the views of an adult in this case are equivalent to the advice of a guardian or guiding spirit. If I try to explain this without going into the spiritual aspects, in short, it means mastering Buddha's teachings.

One of the reasons I always recommend that you should acquire a knowledge of Buddha's Truth is because that knowledge can often help you avoid getting into trouble.

Many people find themselves in difficult situations simply because they do not know the Truth. Imagine an old open well in the ground. If you know where the well is, then you know it is dangerous to go near but if someone does not know the well is there they may fall into it. Using this as a metaphor, the old well is like the views of the majority who live casually and think, 'There is nothing after death', or 'There is no such thing as the other world'. These sorts of people are completely self-indulgent, unaware of the danger in front of them. Inevitably they will fall into the well.

Warning people about the old well implies teaching them that hell really does exist in the other world. It is warning them: 'There is a danger of going to hell, so be careful. Although you are living in this world on Earth at present, there is another world that you will go to after death. If you live in a wrong way, you will have to suffer again in your next life. So live carefully.' To warn people of this danger, our Institute publishes books of Buddha's Truth and holds lectures and seminars. If you are living in a way that brings your mind and your heart into harmony, you will be able to receive inspiration from your guardian spirit.

As I read people's lives through past incarnations, I am able to confirm that each person has particular soul tendencies on the basis of which I can predict to some extent how they will behave and react in certain circumstances. What I predict often matches the way a person actually acts. The person will behave in a certain way, as if their soul was being lured into a particular action. To break this sort of endless cycle, you need to step out of the framework of your own way of thinking and stand at a higher level.

This can also be applied to the subject of management. Confronted with a serious problem, a person of considerable abilities can easily overcome a crisis, while a less able person can easily bring the company to bankruptcy. It is often said that only one person in five succeeds in starting and running their own business. In most cases, failure is not caused by the environment or bad luck, but by someone's lack of ability and managerial skills.

You cannot understand how to manage a business unless you experience and master it by studying, thinking and taking action yourself. Managerial ability is not something that can be inherited or acquired solely through knowledge. This is why inexperienced management causes many companies to go bankrupt every year. However, in many cases, bankruptcies could be prevented if able management consultants were employed, or if advice were available from someone with better managerial skills.

In fact, from a worldly perspective, there are many outstanding people and you may be one of them. However, viewed from one level higher, or from a spiritual point of view, even intelligent people may still be in spiritual darkness. Even if someone seems to have wonderful ability and embodies the highest levels of intelligence in this three-dimensional world, from the viewpoint of the high spirits in the Real World, he or she may know next to nothing.

Someone like this is like an ant being kept alive in a miniature garden. The ant may be proud of its expert knowledge of the miniature garden in the box, but the fact is that the ant has been captured by a human being and is being kept inside a box. This ant, so proud of its expertise in one miniature garden is like a person who seems to excel in worldly abilities. Of course, this ant is certainly cleverer than the others who do not have its expert knowledge as it is capable of avoiding potential dangers. This metaphor can be applied to those living in the three-dimensional world.

4

Criteria for Identifying True Religion – Self-Reflection and Self-Responsibility

As I have already explained, karma is formed by the choices you make according to the tendencies of your mind and heart, and the actions you take on the basis of your judgements. Karma will remain on the record of your life and will also influence future incarnations. It can also be expressed in inclinations.

In the light of this truth, one subject we must look into concerns the current activities of different religious groups. It is not only new religious organisations, but also traditional groups which often employ the term 'karma' and they usually use it in a way that implies only negative karma. Many misguided religious groups speak of the karma of ancestors, grandparents, parents, siblings, and so on. According to these groups, karma of this kind will bring you misfortune so you must get rid of it. Misfortune is often attributed to an ancestor's karma and people are persuaded to hold a ritualised service to get rid of it. But no matter how much you pay for a ritual to be performed, if it is based on wrong ideas it will not have much effect.★

It is actually very possible that among the members of your family, there is a soul who has been unable to return to heaven. It may be your father, your mother, a grandparent or someone from a previous generation. If you trace back carefully, you will always find these sorts of souls in a family lineage. In theory, this can have an influence on the descendants.

In fact, there is a certain religious organisation that uses this theory to their advantage to justify their practice of performing rituals for ancestors every day. Perhaps this is a variation on the practice of getting rid of negative spiritual influences. Although I teach that it is sometimes true that negative spiritual influences may affect your health or your decisions in a negative way and cause you to suffer, if you discipline your mind, correct your actions and strengthen your physical body, you will be able to free yourself from such influences. I have also said that if you live a righteous and harmonious life on Earth, you are setting an example for ancestors who are suffering in the other world because they lived wrongly on Earth. They may be able to save themselves by following your example.

Let me explain this with the following example. Suppose a father is burdened with a huge debt and his son is also

---

★ See page 136 (my previous footnote about ancestor worship).

burdened with his own equally huge debt. Is it possible for the son to pay off his father's debt when he himself is in debt? The answer is no. If, on the other hand, the son is a successful and wealthy businessman, can he clear his father's debt? The answer is yes. The relationship between ancestors and descendants is exactly the same as the relationship between the father and son in this example. Those ancestors who failed to return to heaven are like people who suffer under a heavy burden of debt. In other words, ancestors suffer on account of the 'spiritual debts' they have incurred during their lives on Earth.

A descendant may have the intention of clearing the 'spiritual debt' of an ancestor so he or she can return to heaven. However, if the descendant is living a corrupt life and is also being spiritually influenced in a negative way, he or she can also be considered to be in debt. A person in debt cannot pay off another person's debt. In order to clear someone else's debt, you must have sufficient savings. Only if you are wealthy can you pay off another person's debt.

'Wealth' in this case means the virtue you have built up in this life on Earth by continuing to achieve spiritual growth daily, based on Buddha's Truth. Only if you have accumulated the virtue of the light of Truth in yourself, or accumulated wealth in heaven, can you offer light to others and share it with people in trouble. This is the correct way of thinking as far as offering services for ancestors is concerned. You cannot save your ancestors simply by offering amulets or performing rituals for them. Instead, it is essential for the descendants who live on Earth to accumulate goodness each day. Provided that they are receiving light from their guardian and guiding spirits by practising the right religious disciplines, they can pray for the happiness of their ancestors and pay off their ancestors' 'debts' using their 'assets' should they wish.

Some people may be tempted to offer to have services for their ancestors in order to release themselves from agonising suffering, for instance illness, financial difficulties or entangled relationships. They think, 'This must be the fault of my ancestors. It is their curse that is the cause of my pain, so if I can drive them far away, I'll get better.' Not only do they fail to drive away the souls of ancestors who are not able to return to heaven, they too go down into the world of darkness. I would like you to take care and steer clear of the commercial ruses of unscrupulous and misguided religions taking advantage of people's anxieties; do not fall victim to them.

Suppose one of your ancestors had gone to prison and you are told that you have a 'karma of imprisonment'. But if you had to go to prison, it would be because you had done something that was against the law; an ancestor would not be responsible. If you claimed that the reason you were in prison was an ancestor's karma of imprisonment that drove you to commit the crime, you would be completely avoiding taking responsibility for yourself. If you were to blame a car accident entirely on the curse of an ancestor's karma and claimed, 'This happened to me because an ancestor once committed a crime,' you would not be taking responsibility for your own thoughts and actions. Or, suppose you got involved in the complications of an amorous relationship and claimed, 'This is because of the curse of my ancestor's karma, the karma of lust, it is not my fault. The problem is that my ancestor couldn't return to heaven, so what I need to do is hold a ritual.' What has happened to taking responsibility for your own mind and actions? There would be no room for you to practise self-reflection.

So, you can judge a religion to be wrong if it denies self-responsibility and self-reflection, and blames ancestors for bad karma. Such a religion may even force you to pay large sums of money on the basis of bad karma. This kind of religion is possessed and being controlled by spirits in hell.

In determining whether a religion is right or wrong you should check to see whether it teaches self-reflection and self-responsibility to those who are living on Earth now and undergoing spiritual discipline. Apply this checkpoint to religious groups which concentrate on performing rituals for ancestors. If they invariably attribute everything to ancestors, saying, 'It is the fault of your ancestors that you cannot lead a happy life', or 'You can live happily on account of the virtue of your ancestors', they are quite wrong. I would like you to understand that both your happiness and your unhappiness are created by you, and that the main mission of religion is to save those people who actually live on this Earth.

5

Group Karma – Shared Destiny

As I have said, karma is essentially connected to taking responsibility for yourself. But there is also the common destiny of an entire society, and the whole of the human race. When there is a major war, people cannot escape its influence, no matter how rightly each individual is living. This phenomenon is referred to as 'group karma' as opposed to the 'individual karma' of each person.

One person may complain, 'Although you say we must not blame our environment, or society, or the age we live in, look at this group karma. Although I didn't want to kill people, a war has broken out and now I have no choice. What do you have to say about this?' or 'Why do I have to suffer in an economic recession even though I work very hard and run my own business?' What you need to remember is that human beings cannot live alone. We cannot live on a desert island in solitude like Robinson Crusoe. We are all part of a community. We must remember we are closely linked with one another by endless chains of cause and effect.

In the light of this, you are at least partially responsible if society is not functioning properly. While your own spiritual development is essential, it is always important to remind yourself that, as a member of your community, your society and your country, you have to do something to create a better world.

To dispel the negative tendencies of our group karma, we need to increase the number of fellow humans who radiate light. We must convey Buddha's Truth to as many people as possible, speaking to every single person with sincerity and enthusiasm. In this way, we will be able to prevent our common destiny and group karma from heading in an unfortunate direction. Now that many catastrophic phenomena are occurring, it is essential that each one of us corrects and refines his or her own mind. But it is an equally important training for us to teach people that each and every person can participate in changing the course of the destiny of the whole of humankind by pursuing their own 'Right Mind'.

To conclude, I would like you to understand deeply that true religion should teach the idea that 'benefiting yourself spiritually benefits others'. It is essential that you guide others while, at the same time, pursuing your own spiritual growth.

Postscript

This book is the third in the 'challenge' series, following on from *The Challenge of Religion* and *The Challenge of Enlightenment*. Buddhism is a philosophy that urges everyone to take on the challenge of their own mind so as to break through the limited potentiality of religion.

I have imbued old Buddhist ideas with new life and these new teachings are based on reason and intellectual understanding, overflowing with a positivity that challenges each and every person. I would like to establish a new philosophy, replacing outdated teachings; with my easy-to-understand explanations, old misguided religious ideas will be pushed aside.

We must deliver religion back into the hands of the true 'elite', the Bodhisattvas or angels of light. The success of the Institute I founded marks the coming of an age when a spiritual 'elite' will be active in society.

Ryuho Okawa
President, the Institute for Research in Human Happiness